Spirituality for Modern Man

Spirituality
for
Modern Man

Edward Carter, S.J.

FIDES PUBLISHERS, INC.
NOTRE DAME, INDIANA

IMPRIMI POTEST: ROBERT F. HARVANEK, S. J.
                  Provincial
                  Chicago Province, Society of Jesus
                  January 1, 1971

NIHIL OBSTAT: EDWARD B. BRUEGGEMAN, S. J.
                  Censor Deputatus

IMPRIMATUR: PAUL F. LEIBOLD
                  Archbishop of Cincinnati
                  January 15, 1971

LCCCN: 71-142907
ISBN: 0-8190-0080-9

The author acknowledges the use of the following copyrighted material:

Excerpts from *The Jerusalem Bible,* copyright © 1966 by Darton, Longman & Todd, Ltd., and Doubleday & Company, Inc. Used by permission of the publisher.

Eucharist, for the contents of Chapter 3 which originally appeared in that magazine.

The Teachings of the Second Vatican Council, Westminster, Maryland: Newman Press, 1966. Used with permission of Paulist/ Newman Press of New York.

From *Theological Dictionary,* by Rahner-Vorgrimler, published by Herder and Herder, 232 Madison Avenue, New York, N.Y. 10016.

From "The Four Moments of Prayer," by John Sheets, S. J., *Review for Religious,* Vol. 28, May, 1969.

To J. G.
Who helps in so many ways

Preface

The spiritual life is not meant to be limited to such formal religious practices as prayer and liturgical participation. Certainly these are important aspects of one's Christian existence, but the spiritual life should somehow also include everything which is really authentically human. Christian spirituality, then, deals with one's total life as guided by the Holy Spirit. The spiritual life is human life in the Spirit. This concept is one of the dominant thrusts contained in the following pages.

Another dominant concept of this book is the fact that the Christian or spiritual life is always a combination of three fundamental elements. It is the Gospel message lived out in the grace of Christ according to one's historical situation. Because of the historically conditioning factor of Christianity, each age of the Church has to rethink for itself how Christianity is to be lived in the here and now. Christian spirituality, consequently, while always remaining essentially the same, is also changing in various ways from age to age. We may legitimately speak of a contemporary spirituality—a spirituality for modern man.

This book is intended for all committed members of the People of God—laity, priests, and religious. It is not a highly systematic and comprehensive view of the spiritual life. We gave this type of presentation in a previous book, *Response in Christ*. The present work takes the theme approach, and each of these themes

vii

carries its own message. Yet there is an inner unity, that provided by the mystery of Christ. To treat of any Christian theme is ultimately to refer to Christ. That the Christian life in one way or the other is always directing itself toward Christ has been well pointed out by St. Paul. He tells us, ". . . and I live now not with my own life but with the life of Christ who lives in me." (Gal 2:20).[1]

The author wishes to take this opportunity to thank all those who in various ways rendered valuable assistance. Very special gratitude is due to Sister Joan Guntzelman, S. C. Special thanks is due to Sister Mary Ann Westhoven, O.P., Father Edward Brueggeman, S. J., and Father William Topmoeller, S. J.

[1] All Scripture quotations are taken from *The Jerusalem Bible* (New York: Doubleday & Company, Inc., 1966).

Contents

I

The Mystery of Christ and Christian Existence

Etymologically, the word *mystery* basically means that which is secret or hidden. It was used in a religiously technical sense even before Christianity. For instance, the word was used to designate certain religious rites of pagan Hellenism, rites closed or secret to outsiders unless they were properly initiated into them. In relation to Egyptian hermeticism the word *mystery* was applied to initiation into secret religious ideas or doctrines.

In reference to Christianity, God himself is the ultimate mystery. Radically, God is completely other and transcendent, hidden in His inner life to man unless He chooses to reveal Himself. He has revealed and communicated Himself to man in Christ. Consequently, the mystery of God becomes the mystery of Christ. In Christ God tells us about Himself, about His inner life, about His plans of creation and redemption. He tells us how He wishes to communicate Himself to us, how He wishes to share with us His own Trinitarian life through grace. All this He has accomplished and does accomplish through Christ. St. Paul tells us: "I became the servant of the Church when God made me responsible for delivering God's message to you, the message which was a mystery hidden for generations and centuries and has now been revealed to his saints. It was God's purpose to reveal it to them and to show all the rich glory of this mystery to pagans. The mystery is Christ among you, your hope of glory: this is the Christ we proclaim, this is the wisdom in which we thoroughly train everyone and instruct everyone, to make them all perfect in Christ." (Col 1:25-28).

It is in and through the human life of Christ that God instructs us and gives Himself to us. God has intimately thrust Himself into human history through the enfleshment of Christ Jesus. In and through the human history of Christ God has spoken to us, has redeemed us, has raised us to a new life. Through the joy, the suffering, the labor, the sense of accomplishment, the frustration, the acceptance and the rejection, the pain and agony, the peace and happiness—all of which comprised the life of Jesus—God was giving Himself to us. The mystery which is God Himself was being revealed to us and shared with us. The mystery of God had become the mystery of Christ: God's concrete plan of redemption through His Incarnate Son.

The life of Christ, then, is the mystery of Christ. The mystery of Christ is the Christ event; it is all the happenings or events of Christ's life, each of which in its own way helped accomplish our redemption. We may speak, consequently, not only of the total, unified mystery of Christ, but also of the individual events or mysteries of Christ's life. True, Christ's mysteries of death and resurrection are central to His redemptive effort, and in some way contain all the other mysteries of His earthly existence. But these other mysteries also have their own importance. In the Rahner-Vorgrimler *Theological Dictionary* we read: "It is not the Incarnation, Cross and Resurrection alone that are of universal significance for the salvation of all . . . The same is true of all the events of Jesus' life. These events are not falsely sublimated or mythologized by being so regarded; we merely recognize that the one total life of Jesus with all it embraces (each detail in its own way and in its own place), deliberately directed to and unified in his death and resurrection, is the one event for the sake of which God is gracious to us . . . The individual events of Jesus' life are therefore always of the same character as his death and resurrection, which are most obviously mysteries. . . ."[1]

The mysteries or events of Jesus' earthly, historical existence are not mere past events. They are still dynamically present in the glorified Christ. How is this so? The mysteries of Christ have a twofold aspect, one historical, limited by time; the other dimension is eternal, perennially and vitally present in Christ.[2] Let us first consider the historical, temporal aspect of Christ's mysteries.

Christ is the entrance of eternity into time, God present among us in human form. The Son in assuming human flesh subjected Himself to the historical dimension of man's existence. In other words, the actions which Christ performed through His human nature here below were limited by temporal historicity. The temporal historicity of these acts cannot be re-enacted, no, not even sacramentally in the liturgy. This would be

[1] Karl Rahner and Herbert Vorgrimler, *Theological Dictionary* (New York: Herder & Herder, 1965), p. 299.
[2] Cf Edward Schillebeeckx, *Christ the Sacrament of the Encounter With God* (New York: Sheed and Ward, 1963), pp. 55–56.

asking God to reproduce a *past* act *now* precisely as *past*, a contradiction in terms.

There is, then, the temporal not-to-be-repeated dimension of Christ's mysteries or life events. However, these mysteries possess another aspect, eternal and perennially dynamic. Christ, although having a divine nature and a human nature, is only one person, and that divine. We see the consequence of this in reference to the acts which Christ performed as man while upon earth. These were acts of a divine person and therefore share in the eternity of the divine person Who is above the historical, temporal limitations of earthly space and time. The events of Christ's historical existence truly endure eternally in the glorified Christ, and they endure for a purpose.

The mysteries or events of Christ's life perennially endure in Him to be assimilated by men, especially by the members of the People of God. We are thus saved and sanctified by entering into the mystery of Christ, assimilating it, and reproducing it in our own lives according to our particular vocations, graces, and historical exigencies. There is radically only one manner of life which the Father holds before us, that patterned after the existence of His Incarnate Son. St. John tells us this: "We can be sure that we are in God only when the one who claims to be living in him is living the same kind of life as Christ lived." (I Jn 2:5-6). And St. Paul also reminds us that we must be formed after the image of Christ: "We know that by turning everything to their good God co-operates with all those who love him, with all those that he has called according to his purpose. They are the ones he chose specially long ago and intended to become true images of his Son, so that his Son might be the eldest of many brothers." (Rm 8:28-29).

By reliving and reincarnating the mysteries of Christ, the People of God are not only accomplishing their own redemption, but are assisting in the continued application of Christ's redemption to all men. The Incarnation continues on for all time. Christ, of course, is He Who has become Incarnate, and He is the One Who fundamentally continues the Incarnation. But He enlists our help. The world no longer sees Christ, no longer is able to reach out and touch Him. We are the ones who now in some way make Christ visible and tangible, existentially present to the world of men. In union with the invisible, glorified Christ, and drawing upon Him as our source of strength, we continue the Incarnation in its visible and temporal dimensions. The fact that we do this poorly at times because of our human weakness and sinfulness does not change the great privilege and responsibility which is ours—we, the People of God, do help continue the Incarnation. We are the Body of Christ. We are the mystical Christ. The People of God must continue to reincarnate the mystery and mysteries of Christ. It is true that the Church and the Christian do not help reincarnate Christ in exactly the same way from age to age. The Church of the Second Vatican Council is not the same Church as that of the Reformation and post-Tridentine age. The Christian of today is not in every manner the same as the second century Christian. The Church and her people are rightfully caught up into the dynamic and changing evolution of man and his world. Thus, although Church and Christian will always help to continue the Incarnation in the same essential manner, there will be differences from age to age. But the basic and wonderful reality is always with us: the mystery of Christ continues to be reincarnated through His members.

6 SPIRITUALITY FOR MODERN MAN

We must be careful to remember that the mystery of Christ, or the life of Christ, is continued by the People of God in a very human way, as well as in a divine, supernatural way. This was the manner in which Christ lived. Christ as man redeemed us through actions which were elevated and divinized by His life of grace. (We here remind the reader that Christ as man possessed His own life of sanctifying grace.) But these elevated, divinized actions of Christ were also *human* actions. To put it another way, the redemptive acts of Christ remained human actions although they were elevated to a new level of existence through grace. With these points understood we can state that Christ lived out His salvific events or mysteries within the framework of an ordinary human existence, that of the Jewish world of His times. Christ lived out His mysteries amid the human experiences which are a part of any man's existence. Christ shared deep, love-filled family relationships with Mary and Joseph at Nazareth. He experienced joy when the little children flocked to Him in their fresh and uninhibited innocence. He felt satisfaction and a sense of accomplishment when His apostles responded, however slowly, to the mission He intended for them. He enjoyed the friendship of Martha, Mary, and Lazarus. His sensitive nature thrilled at the beauty and wonder of His Father's creation—at the simple magnificence of the lilies of the field, at the cool and refreshing night breeze, at the raging strength of a stormy wind.

Christ also experienced the other side of human existence. He experienced pain, and sorrow, and disappointment, and loneliness, and rejection, and misunderstanding, and spiritual anguish. This darker side of Christ's life reached its heart-rending culmination upon Calvary. There He hung upon a cross, an apparent failure to the eyes of man, a tragic failure, His life being crushed out by the shameful death of crucifixion. He hung there, rejected by His Jewish People, betrayed by Judas, denied by Peter, abandoned by His apostles. Then suddenly came the intense joy of the resurrection. Christ in His brief life span had more or less ranged the gamut of human experiences. The Christ event, the mystery of Christ, had truly been lived out in a human way, within the framework of the human condition.

The Church relives and continues the Christ event in a similar manner. The Church lives a new existence in Christ, it is true: "And for anyone who is in Christ, there is a new creation; the old creation has gone, and now the new one is here." (2 Co 5:17). But this new life in Christ does not destroy anything which is authentically human. It rather elevates it, perfects it, shoots it through with a new vitality and dynamism. The People of God, collectively and individually, are meant to be more human precisely because they live in Christ. It is not by rejecting what is really human that the Church relives Christ's mysteries and continues the Incarnation; it is rather by living the authentically human in a higher mode of existence—in Christ—that Church and Christian relive and continue the Christ event. As Christ worked out His redemptive Incarnation within the framework of an ordinary human existence, likewise do Church and Christian help to continue that Incarnation which is the mystery of Christ.

The Incarnation continued, consequently, is the People of God going about their daily lives in Christ; it is their living the really human, whatever this may be in the concrete, existential situation, as permeated with love of God and man as guided by the Father's will.

The Incarnation continued and made visible upon this earth is, then, for instance, the Christian family experiencing together the joy and the suffering, the work and the relaxation, the challenges and accomplishments, the hopes and the fears, of human existence. The Christ event continued is the young boy, his leg recently amputated because of cancer, trying to be brave but afraid in the depths of his young heart that the hopes and dreams of future years will never be his. The Incarnation continued is the loneliness which cuts through, very deeply at times, so many human hearts. The here and now Christ event is a young Christian couple, walking hand in hand, vibrant with the freshness of their love and in wonderment at its mystery. The Incarnation still with us is all the particular joys and difficulties peculiar to the various states of life, priestly, religious and lay. The life of Christ continued is the work of scholars, technicians, doctors, scientists, industrialists, and the common laborer, as all contribute in accord with their own skills to the betterment of man and his earthly city. The mystery of Christ among us is the members of the Church striving to adapt themselves to the needs of the time in a strange mixture of conservatism and liberalism, high idealism and sinfulness, efficiency and ineptness, courage and cowardice. In summary, the Incarnation continued in its visible, this-world dimension is human existence as elevated by Christ; it is mankind, especially the People of God, experiencing all the varied dimensions of the human condition in Christ.

The Christian is initiated into the mystery of Christ, into his role of prolonging the Incarnation, through baptism. In the words of St. Paul: "You have been taught that when we were baptised in Christ Jesus we were baptised in his death; in other words, when we were baptised we went into the tomb with him and joined him in death, so that as Christ was raised from the dead by the Father's glory, we too might live a new life . . . Christ, as we know, having been raised from the dead will never die again. Death has no power over him any more. When he died, he died, once for all, to sin, so his life now is life with God; and in that way, you too must consider yourselves to be dead to sin but alive for God in Christ Jesus." (Rm 6:3-11). Let us remember that as we are baptised into Christ's death and resurrection, we are also baptised into the other mysteries of Christ. The total mystery of Christ is profoundly unified. To be incorporated into any one part of it is to be simultaneously incorporated into each and every part or individual mystery.

It is not sufficient that we be incorporated into Christ and His mysteries through baptism. As with any form of life, our life in Christ must be continually nourished once it has been originally received. We must constantly keep in contact with Christ and His mysteries if our Christ-life is to grow properly. How can we continually encounter Christ? There are various ways. We contact Christ in a special manner through the liturgy, and above all in the Eucharistic liturgy. Here the entire course of salvation history as centered in the mystery of Christ is sacramentally renewed and continued. Through this Eucharistic encounter the members of the People of God are more deeply incorporated into all the various mysteries of Christ.

The reading of Sacred Scripture provides another special opportunity for encounter with Christ. This is true for both the Old and New Testaments, for the Old prefigures the New and leads to it. However, as is obvious, we meet Christ and His mysteries very especially through the pages of the New Testament. How true it is to say that not to be familiar with Scripture is not to know Christ properly.

There is still another special way in which we make encounter with the mysteries of Christ. We make renewed contact with Jesus and His mysteries as these are present within us and others. Through our grace-life Christ and His mysteries are truly and wonderfully with us. The mysteries of Christ, as to be relived by us, are structured into our life of grace. One of the best ways, then, to encounter the mysteries or events of Christ's life is to *experience* these personally and existentially in our own Christian living. To relive the mysteries of Christ is to understand them more perfectly, and, in turn, this deeper penetration of their truth allows for their still greater assimilation in our lives.

And to see the truth of Christ, the Christ event, reincarnated to a marked degree in another person—what a gift of God this is. To a large extent Christianity has failed to impress the world as it should because it is only in a relatively few lives that we see the mystery of Christ renewed and continued. To see the selflessness of Christ, His love, His kindness, His gentleness, His willingness to suffer and endure the difficult, His joy and peace despite the pain and anguish of life—to see all this of Christ reflected in the lives of at least some of those we meet, this is a magnificent encounter with Christ, His truth, His mystery.

And let us remember that we make contact with Christ's mysteries in ourselves and others not just as individuals, but also as members of a covenant, the People of God, and as members of the community of man in general. One of our greatest experiences in reliving the Christ event can be the mutual sharing and living of this event with others in various types of personal relationships and encounters. For example, the demand which selfless love makes upon man and wife is an experience of God's agape or selfless love made visible and incarnate to us in Christ.

The joy, the unitive force, and even ecstasy at times, of married love, or of the love of friendship, is another experience of the Christ event. Christ came principally to give us a new life of love, and by His own life He showed us how to love and open ourselves to receive love. Personal relationships, not only with the divine persons, but with human persons also, provide one of the best schools for learning and assimilating this aspect of Christ's mystery.

Common to the various ways of properly encountering Christ and His mysteries is a certain degree of prayerful reflection. Our encounter with the mystery of Christ in the liturgy, Scripture, ourselves and others will never be reasonably ideal without this kind of reflection. Faith and love are the two principal Christian virtues we exercise in assimilating Christ's mysteries wherever encountered. The faith aspect of this encounter demands that we reflect meaningfully and prayerfully on the Christ event, seeing what it is in Christ Himself and how it is to be incorporated into our own Christian existence.

There are, then, numerous ways in which we meet Christ in His mysteries. The privilege and the responsibility of the Christian is to strive to grow in the understanding and the reliving of the mystery of Christ. If the Christian acts in this manner he achieves an ever-increasing insight concerning what Jesus tells us: "I am the Way, the Truth, and the Life." (Jn 14:6).

2

The Meaning
of Christ's Enfleshment

The Christian life is rooted in the great event of the Incarnation. We must always focus our gaze on Christ, realizing that everything the Father wishes to tell us has been summed up in the life of Jesus of Nazareth.

Before we direct our attention to the human enfleshment of the Word, let us first briefly consider His existence from all eternity in God Himself. The Father from all eternity, in a perfect act of self-expression, in a perfect act of knowing, generates His Son. The Son, the Word, is, then, the immanent expression of God's fulness, the perfect reflection and image of the Father, the divine exemplar after which all creation is in some way fashioned. And from all eternity the Father and His Word, His Son, in a perfect act of love bring forth the Holy Spirit.

At the destined moment in human history, God's self-expression, the Word, immersed Himself into man's world. God's inner self-expression now had also become God's self-expression outside of Himself. Through the Incarnation of the Word God had become so intimately with us. The Word truly had become flesh and He lived in our midst, and the cost of it all He did not count: "In your minds you must be the same as Christ Jesus: His state was divine, yet he did not cling to his equality with God but emptied himself to assume the condition of a slave, and became as men are; and being as all men are, he was humbler yet, even to accepting death, death on a cross." (Ph 2:5-8).

Through the Incarnation the Father has definitively spoken. It only remains for us to fathom ever more deeply the inexhaustible truth of the Word Incarnate. Yes, the Father has definitively spoken to us in Christ, telling us about Himself and His gracious design for us: "At various times in the past and in various different ways, God spoke to our ancestors through the prophets; but in our own time, the last days, he has spoken to us through his Son, the Son that he has appointed to inherit everything and through whom he made everything there is." (Heb 1:1-2).

This Word made flesh is light come into darkness, all-powerful to lead the world from sinfulness to its true destiny. The Christmas liturgy, using the words of the book of Wisdom, tells us: "When peaceful silence lay over all, and night had run the half of her swift course, down from the heavens, from the royal throne, leapt your all-powerful Word. . ." (Ws 18:14-15).

What was the condition of man and his world at the time of Christ's coming? In one way, people were much the same as we are today. There were those just being born into this world of human drama; there were those who in death were leaving it, some of whom had not begun to understand the purpose of human existence. There were those who were healthy and vigorous; others were sick and lame. Some felt especially the burdens, the grief, the suffering of the human condition;

others were ebullient and alive with the desire for all pleasures life could provide. There was some good being accomplished, especially in such great centers as Rome with her genius for government and architecture, and in Athens with her philosophers, writers, sculptors and artists. But the moral condition of those times was at a very low ebb. What St. Paul tells us of that time shortly following Christ's earthly existence certainly must be applied also at His entrance into the world. It is an ugly picture that Paul depicts for us: "The anger of God is being revealed from heaven against all the impiety and depravity of men who keep truth imprisoned in their wickedness. . . That is why God has abandoned them to degrading passions: why their women have turned from natural intercourse to unnatural practices and why their menfolk have given up natural intercourse to be consumed with passion for each other. . . . And so they are steeped in all sorts of depravity, rottenness, greed and malice, and addicted to envy, murder, wrangling, treachery and spite. Libellers, slanderers, enemies of God, rude, arrogant and boastful, enterprising in sin, rebellious to parents, without brains, honour, love or pity. They know what God's verdict is: that those who behave like this deserve to die—and yet they do it; and what is worse, encourage others to do the same." (Rm 1:18-32).

Into such a depraved condition of mankind Christ entered, with a full and generous heart, to lead man from the depths of his sinfulness to the vibrant richness of a new life in Himself. This Christ had become through His enfleshment the focal point of all history. All the authentic hopes and dreams of all ages, now overshadowed so deeply by the ugliness of sin, came converging upon this Christ. He would gather them up in Himself, give them a new lustre and brilliance and dynamism, and would lead the renewed human race back to the Father in the Spirit.

Christ came, then, for a double purpose, or rather for a single purpose with two facets. He was radically to release us from the dominion of sin and to elevate us to a new level of existence. This life which Christ has given us, traditionally termed the supernatural life, is not a type of superstructure erected atop man's normal life. The Christian is not one-half natural and one-half supernatural. He is one graced person. In his entirety he has been raised up, caught up, into a deeper form of life in Christ Jesus. Nothing which is authentically human has been excluded from this new existence. Whatever is really human in the life of the Christian is meant to be both an expression and a growth of the Christ-life. The simple but deep joys of family life, the wonderment at nature's beauty, the kiss which unites lovers, the warm embrace of a mother for her child, the agony of crucial decision-making, the success or frustration experienced in one's work, the joy of being well-received by others, and the heart-ache of being misunderstood, everything—yes, all dimensions of the Christian's life, sin alone excepted—is meant to be caught up in Christ and made more deeply human because of Him.

Christ has come, not to destroy anything which is really human, but to perfect it by leading it to a graced fulfillment. This is the meaning of the Incarnation. Christ, who is God, has been bold and daring enough to live a God-like existence. In a seeming paradox, the more God-like we become through grace, the more human we become; for the grace-life is the living of a human life in a higher way, a more vital way. The road to an ever greater participation in this new life, it is true, is not always smoothly paved. The Christ-life is very difficult at times, but it is man's only complete fulfillment. If the world is still plagued with so much that should not be, we must look for the answer in the direction pointed out by Chesterton, who, somewhat exaggerating for the sake of emphasis, has stated that, "The Christian ideal has not been tried and found wanting. It has been found difficult; and left untried." Christ has done His part, and to the extent that we respond to Him we realize with a greater penetration of mind and heart the meaning of His words: "I have come so that they may have life and have it to the full." (Jn 10:10).

The life which Christ has given us is centered in love. It has its origins in the mysterious love of God, His agape, through which He so selflessly achieves His self-communication to men, drawing them and their world so intimately to Himself: "Yes, God loved the world so much that he gave his only Son, so that everyone who believes in him may not be lost but may have eternal life." (Jn 3:16). Not only has our new life in Christ arisen out of God's fathomless love, but its entire dynamism breathes love. The Incarnate Word Himself has taught us this. In our behalf He has as man perfectly opened Himself to being possessed by the Father's love; He in turn has responded to the Father in love. In relation to men, Christ has loved completely and fully from the depths of His being, pouring Himself out in a life of selfless service, a self-giving which drew from Him life's breath itself so that He could say He loved, and without reserve, and to the end. Thus forever was etched upon the pages of man's history, indelibly and so deeply, the love of Christ for His brothers. In this very greatness and depth of Christ's love for men,

He was also opening Himself to their love, for Christ can enter the human heart only if there is a response of love to encounter His own. Consequently, in His Incarnation Christ is the sacrament—the visible sign—of the four great dimensions of Christian love. The Christian is he who receives God's love and responds with his own love, one who loves his fellow-men, and, in turn, opens himself to receive their love.

Christ, in His descent into human flesh, has established a milieu of love. The life He came to give can flourish only in the framework of love. Love is the beginning and it is the end. This life of Christian love is nuanced in various ways. Our love is lived amid the joy of being possessed by God, or amid the erroneous fear of being too much possessed by Him. Christian love can be experienced as the exhilaration of fresh married love; or at times its exercise must take place in the crushing experience of being rejected by the very one deeply loved. And pain and sorrow and peace and happiness—these and other experiences are also present in the life of Christian love, and the ebb and flow of all of these are as varying as life itself. But the one main truth which must be grasped is that the redemptive Incarnation was wrought by God's love to raise us in turn to a deeper level of loving. Our deeper penetration into the mystery of the Incarnation can take place only in love. Incarnate love can only be understood and participated in more fully through our own growth in love.

There are other truths connected with the Incarnation besides that of love. One of these is personalism. There were numerous possibilities open to God, given His decision to redeem the human race. Yet what plan did He actually choose? He accomplished our redemption in the most personalistic way. He communicated Himself anew to us through the personal enfleshment of His Son. Once the Incarnation had taken place, it was through the human life of Jesus that God was continually communicating Himself to us. This means that God was giving Himself to us through the warmth, the kindness, the strength, the gentleness, the selflessness which emanated from the Incarnate person Christ. The personalism of the Incarnation means that the various dimensions which make up a human life were, through the human life of Jesus, channeling God's self-communication to us. It was truly the incarnate, personal acts of Christ that redeemed us—His work and relaxation, His joy, His friendships, His love for Mary and Joseph, His training of the apostles, His concern for the most abject of those He encountered, His fatigue, His agony and death, His resurrection—all personalistic acts, the personal acts of the one called Jesus. Our redemption, it was all so personalistic.

The personalism of the Incarnation continues on. We, the People of God, in union with Christ, are called upon to help Christ continue His Incarnation in its visible, earthly dimension. There is only one framework available to us according to which we help further the Incarnation. It is that of our personal lives, that of individuals united together as a people, the People of God. It is the human condition as we experience it, joyfully, and painfully, too, that provides the soil for our participation in the continued Incarnation. It is not by trying to remove ourselves from the human condition, but by striving to live the authentically human more and more in Christ that redemption continues to take place. It is by living truly personalistic lives, that is, lives springing forth from the greatness of the person as created by God, lives which do not flinch from the human condition, that redemption continues to be made visible to this world.

We help prolong the Incarnation above all by our personal relationships with God, with members of the People of God, and with others, too. Here again Christ has shown the way. Through the Word made flesh the life of the Trinity has incarnationally manifested itself to men. The life of the Trinity centers in the personal relationships between Father, Son and Holy Spirit. God's life is also His love gone out to the human race. The Incarnation projects this Trinitarian life into the spatial and the temporal. Christ has come to tell us about God's Trinitarian life, to give us a share in it, to teach us that through grace we share in God's life—a life of relationships—by entering into deepened personal relationships with God and human persons. Redemption received and contributed to is essentially the experience of the above-mentioned relationships. Here is where Christian faith, hope and love are chiefly exercised. Redemption continued is the blind trust in God which allows me to accomplish things which are totally beyond my natural courage. It is the growing abandonment, despite possible fear, to the love of God. Redemption continued is loving those afar off whom I will never see or know, but whom I know are my brothers, and whom my work and prayer can reach out and touch, even though I personally cannot. Redemption continued is the Christian hope and trust which allows man and woman to take the risk of the mutual self-giving which is marriage. Redemption continued is the black man who continues to relate to his white brother in faith, hope and love despite his temptations to hatred and bitterness. Redemption continued is the thrill of being loved deeply by another human being; it is also the ecstasy and the agony of myself deeply loving another. Truly, the Incarnation visibly continued essentially is our Christian faith, hope and love made alive in our personal relationships with God and man. In the time of the historical Christ-event, the Incarnation was achieved through the "personalism" of Christ, a personalism centered in Christ's loving relationship with His Father and man. The Incarnation, in its visible, earthly manifestation, is meant to continue in the same fashion.

We have observed that the Incarnation teaches us about love and the personalistic. It teaches us a further truth also. It teaches us the value of the created, the material, the tangible, in God's plan of redemption. The Incarnation established a set pattern for the redemption of the world, redemption taken both objectively (the historical, salvific life of Christ) and subjectively (the redemption as applied to men). Christ redeemed the world through His humanity, a created and tangible reality. As Christ's humanity was indispensable for accomplishing the objective redemption, likewise necessary are created things for continuing the redemption subjectively. In speaking of the place of material creation in the Eucharistic liturgy, Vagaggini succinctly points at the value of everything material: "It is in the Eucharist that material creation finds its noblest use. The changing of bread and wine into Christ's body and blood is the most extraordinary elevation and transfiguration of the material world to the service of the divine life. Aside from the assumption of a human body by the Son of God, there is no more wonderful example of the importance of the role played by this world in the divine plan."[1] This statement of

[1] C. Vagaggini, *Theological Dimensions of the Liturgy* (Collegeville: Liturgical Press, 1959), pp. 181–182.

Vagaggini calls to mind the thought of Teihard de Chardin. Teilhard holds a world concept in which all things, natural and supernatural, spiritual and material, are united in a single and organic unity. The pole of this unity is the person of the Incarnate Word towards Whom the whole of creation converges.[2]

The views of Vagaggini and Teilhard and of others like them are based upon solid theological fact. In assuming human nature, Christ has united to Himself not only all men, but also man's material world. The whole temporal order is caught up into the new dynamism of the redemptive Incarnation. The Second Vatican Council tells us: "Christ's work of redemption is directed both toward the salvation of men as individuals, and at the renewal of the whole secular order."[3]

Not only man's spirit, but also his body and his material world have been given a new dignity because of the Incarnation. These enter so vitally into the Incarnation continued. Once for all let us lay aside the errors of Manichaeism, Neo-Platonism and similar false teachings which deprecate that which is material. We are not claiming that we always use the created and material properly. We misuse these at times, sometimes frequently. At such times we have failed to be related to the material according to God's will. Christ, in elevating the material to a new dignity, has accomplished this partially through that part of the Incarnation which is the cross. The cross dimension of the Incarnation as well as its other aspects must also be present in our encounter with the material. We must realize that such

[2] Cf P. Teilhard de Chardin, *The Divine Milieu* (New York: Harper and Row, 1965), p. 114.

[3] *Decree on the Apostolate of the Laity,* No. 5. All quotations from the Second Vatican Council Documents are taken from *The Teachings of the Second Vatican Council* (New York: Newman Press, 1966).

elements as Christian self-discipline and renunciation must find a place in our lives if we are to use things material according to the divine plan.

There are numberless applications of the value of the material, the visible, the tangible, in our Christ-lives. Vagaggini's reference to material creation and the Eucharist is only one of these applications. In so many ways that which is material, visible and tangible nourishes the Christian life. There is the inspiring homily, the warm, receptive smile of a friend, the reading of Scripture, the physical love of man and wife, the exhilarating refreshment of a day at the seashore, God's loveliness reflected in a little child—and the list could go on and on. The fundamental principle is the same in all cases. The human nature of Christ, something created and material, has reached out and touched all these other things and experiences which are part of life in a material world. When properly related to, they are extensions of the Incarnation for us. They are the redemptive Incarnation applied to us. They are also opportunities for us to help Christ continue His Incarnation for others.

The Incarnation, as we have briefly pointed out, was and is a rich and varied event. The truths which accompany Christ's descent into our world are numerous, capable not only of originally elevating us to a new and vital life, but of constantly leading us to a deeper, richer, and more vibrant participation in that life. This is why Christ came to live in our midst—to give us life and to give it more abundantly. "The Word was made flesh, he lived among us . . ." (Jn 1:14).

3

Life in the
Changing Church

Every Catholic realizes that the Church is in a period of change, a change which is touching practically every dimension of her existence. There are various reactions to this change. Some think that it is happening too quickly, or that there is too much of it. Others believe there is too little change being too slowly implemented. Still others are of the opinion that there is just about the proper degree of change taking place at just about the proper pace. And all would probably agree that, in one way or another, the period of change has been accompanied by an unique type of suffering.

All of us should try to understand the truths and principles pertaining to change in the Church. If we are among those who relate positively to the current changes and approve of them in general, we can still be helped if we know something of the truths and principles according to which legitimate change takes place. If we are among those who are upset by the changes, then we can be helped by seeing the reasons why there actually must be a certain change always occurring in the Church.

What are some of these truths which shed light on the dimension of change in today's Church? First of all, let us look directly at the Incarnation itself. The Son of God assumed a human nature, or became a man, at a certain time in history, in a certain part of the world, and among a certain people. The consequence of all this was that He fundamentally adapted His message according to the historical situation into which His human enfleshment had placed Him. He lived like a Jewish man of the times. He preached His message according to the thought and speech categories proper to the then-existent Jewish culture. Briefly, Christ adapted His message to the life situation of His hearers without in any way compromising it.

The Church, which is the earthly, visible continuation of the Incarnation, must, after the example of Christ, her Head, adapt her message and life according to the general historical milieu in which she is situated. She must do this without falsely compromising the truth entrusted to her by Christ. Admittedly, to adapt without compromising is at times a very difficult task, but it is a task which the Church must always courageously confront.

We can approach the question of change in the Church from the perspective of another truth of the Incarnation. This particular truth is closely linked to that of adaptation just mentioned, but it has its own nuance. It deals with what Christ assumed. Through His own unique human enfleshment Christ also assumed or united to Himself all of mankind and all the authentic and various dimensions of man's existence. One of these dimensions is the fact that man in part is an historically evolving creature. True, he is always essentially the same from age to age. But in many ways he is changing and evolving. The economic structure of twentieth century man is vastly more developed and sophisticated than it was in the ancient days of the barter system. And so it is for all the different aspects of man's existence—political, scientific, sociological, recreational, and the rest—these have changed and evolved through history. The Church in her dealings with men must take all of this into consideration. She must accept men as she finds them in their present stage of evolvement and change. Otherwise the Church would be serving man from the position of an ivory tower which is closed off from man as he actually is in his contemporary world. The essentials of Christianity are the same century after century, but the Church has to attempt to present and channel these essentials in a manner which can change considerably with the times. (The renewed liturgy demonstrates this. The liturgy is constituted by unchangeable elements divinely instituted, but also by elements which the Church can change.) In other words, the unchanging Christian essentials are perpetuated through means and structures which permit a certain variation. Proper change in the Church, then, meets the needs of a changing world. A Church willing to change recognizes the fact that Christ in His Incarnation has assumed the changing evolutionary character of man and therefore respects man in change as He channels the fruits of His Incarnation to mankind in its historical development.

We would like to discuss another truth which has bearing on change in the Church. This particular truth deals with the Church as the on-going, visible manifestation of Christ's life, a life rich in its variety and perfections. Yes, it is the task of the Church to continue to reflect Christ insofar as she can. Immediately we see that this is an endless process, for the Church could never perfectly mirror forth Christ even though she existed a million years. Because of the richness and variety contained in Christ, we can understand why the Church from age to age can very possibly emphasize now this aspect of Christ's message and life, now that aspect—and this implies a certain type of change. For example, in the ages of special persecution the Church has given a vivid witness to the Christ Who was beaten, ridiculed, and finally put to death. In our present day Church we are stressing, among other things, the value of community. We are perhaps more aware than certain previous ages that Christ through His redemptive work intended to form a People of God united to one another as closely as possible through mutual bonds of love.

But is it not only in her successive ages that the Church gives special and varied witness to this or that aspect of the mystery of Christ. Within one and the same age the Church is always witness to a certain diversity or pluralism. The various schools of spirituality associated with the different religious orders are a good example of this. The Benedictine spirituality gives special witness to the priesthood of Jesus as it very obviously centers itself around the liturgy. Franciscan spirituality gives a special emphasis to the material simplicity and poverty of Christ's life upon earth. The Carmelite spirituality has always stressed prayer, as it mirrors forth the Christ Who often prayed to His heavenly father. And so likewise for the spiritualities of the other religious orders. While all are professing the same basic following of the Christ of the Gospels, they do maintain their own particular emphasis in the imitation of Christ.

Today's Church gives a special witness to the pluralism through which the Church can project the varied richness of Christ's life and message. One of the more difficult truths we have to adjust to in the contemporary Church is that this diversity in living out the mystery of Christ is possible in so many different ways. We are witnessing in today's changing Church a diversified life-style and thought-style that perhaps have not been equaled in past ages. This is a challenge, for it demands a greater maturity than would be required if there were much less diversity in the Church. Certainly this diversity must exist and be guided by the truth of Christ and must be respectful of legitimate authority. If these conditions are present, then we should welcome diversity in the Church with its accompanying changes, for such diversity better reflects the total richness and varied perfection of Christ's life and teaching.

One example of this diversity in today's Church is that connected with the conservative-liberal polarity we are all so much aware of. We should all try to be deeply convinced that the Church has need of different classes—the more conservative, and the more liberal, for instance. The more liberal are needed to insure that the Church will change, adapt and progress as God intends. The more conservative are needed to help insure that the unchangeable elements of the Church's life always receive proper attention, and that the change that does take place is properly implemented. As long as both conservative and liberal are open to the guidance of the Holy Spirit, both are vital to a healthy Church.

There is, then, an authentic type of change based on sound theology, a change which is not only good but even necessary in the life of the Church. Yet we all realize that not all the changes taking place in our contemporary Church are legitimate and good. Some are abusing the freedom of this present period of Church change and renewal. Changes which are really not inspired by the Holy Spirit are accompanying the changes which are legitimate, and sometimes it is difficult for us to discern the difference. While we are grieved at this mixture of good and bad change, we must strive to view the situation in proper perspective. We must realize that any gift of God is open to abuse. There is not one gift God has given man that has not been misused. How many times has one of these most basic gifts, man's free will, been misused? Numberless times, we all well know. Just as God does not refuse to give His gifts even though He knows they will be abused at times, so too we should not fail to welcome the realities of change and renewal in the Church although we realize that there will be concomitant abuses.

We are experiencing a certain suffering in our contemporary Church because we do not relish seeing these abuses. This is one type of pain or suffering connected with Church renewal. There are other kinds also. There is that suffering which some experience as they see former elements or structures of the Church's life change or disappear. Having cherished these elements or structures and having derived a type of security from them, people of this sort naturally suffer to some extent as the waves of renewal change previous practices and structures. There is also a pain or suffering involved in the uncertainty accompanying our age of change. It is not always easy to discern just where the Spirit is really breathing amid the diversity of life-style and thought-style in today's Church. This uncertainty can cause us to suffer, even to suffer deeply at times.

But in the midst of the suffering involved with change and renewal, we should strive to maintain our substantial peace of soul. We must learn to suffer as the saints of the Church have. We must suffer while maintaining a true peace of mind, and a Christian joy and happiness and optimism. We must realize that the pattern of death and resurrection which was at the center of Christ's earthly existence is at the center of the Church's and the Christian's existence. Just as Christ achieved the new existence of the resurrection for Himself and mankind through suffering and death, so too the People of God, individually and collectively, will achieve a greater grace life—a greater share in Christ's resurrection—only if they are willing to bear with hardship and suffering. The hardship and the suffering are not ends in themselves, just as they were not in Christ's life. In our lives they are means to that which is most positive—a greater Christ-life of faith, hope, and love. Part of the suffering we must bear today as we strive to grow in Christ is that linked with change and renewal.

And one final suggestion—as we go about our task of adapting the Church's life to contemporary times, let us not think that change means complete upheaval, that we always have to be making more or less completely fresh starts. No kind of life develops in this manner. All life builds upon the past in various ways. The Church's life authentically develops or evolves by allowing the essential and timeless values to be wedded properly to contemporary changes. We must listen to the Master, Our Lord Jesus. He has something to say about blending the old and the new. In the Gospel of Saint Matthew we hear Jesus speak: "And he said to them, 'Well, then, every scribe who becomes a disciple of the kingdom is like a householder who brings out from his storeroom things both new and old'." (Mt 13:52).

4

A Spirituality
for Times of Uncertainty

The experience of various kinds of uncertainty is an inescapable part of life. It is part of man's burden to have to confront courageously and endure patiently the pain attached to uncertainty. The list of examples of human uncertainty is endless. There is that connected with the approach of a first experience. An expectant mother about to give birth to her first child is particularly anxious because she has not gone through it all before and she is uncertain as to what the experience will actually be like. The young doctor in training is understandably apprehensive as he prepares for his first surgery. He is uncertain whether or not he will perform competently under the pressure of the operating room.

There are also so many other kinds of uncertainty. The fighting man agonizes over the uncertainty of when and where the enemy will be encountered. The young man and woman to be married quite suddenly begin to realize the uncertainties connected with marriage. Am I really marrying the right person? Will the children born be normal and healthy? Will my partner love me over a lifetime, or is it possible that love will turn to coldness or even hatred? The young business man—he too can be heavily burdened by the shadow of uncertainty. He anxiously wonders whether this particular financial investment will be a source of great earnings for his company or ultimately lead to bankruptcy. And there is that common uncertainty which has plagued all men of our contemporary age: will life as we now know it upon this earth end so suddenly in an atomic holocaust?

The Christian experiences the kind of uncertainties we have been describing to the same extent as does his non-Christian brother. After all, both share alike the same human condition. Yet the Christian, precisely because he is a Christian, should react to uncertainty and assimilate it in a manner which will differ from that of the non-Christian. One's Christian life is supposed to extend to all the dimensions of authentic human existence, whether it be the experience of uncertainty or anything else.

There is another way in which the Christian experiences uncertainty in a manner different from the non-Christian. We here are referring to those uncertainties which explicitly arise out of one's Christian belief and practice. Some of these uncertainties are common to the Christian regardless of the age of the Church in which he lives. Others are more peculiar to his own historical situation—whether he is living in a sixteenth century Church or a post-Vatican II Church. First let us look at various uncertainties which accompany the Christian life in any age.

Perfect certitude rarely accompanies Christian living. A certain minimal degree of uncertainty in the following of Christ is to a greater or lesser extent always with us. Here, though, we wish to speak of deeper states of uncertainty which confront the Christian from time to time. Examples of such uncertainty are numerous. It may be a case of deciding one's basic state of life. The doubt, confusion and anxiety which can temporarily accompany a choice of vocation can be agonizingly painful for some people. And as one lives out his vocation there may be innumerable decisions which have to be made in a cloud of uncertainty. These decisions often involve others besides ourselves. This fact adds to the difficulty. Not knowing what will be all the various consequences of our decisions—the uncertain future which our decisions will bring upon us—this, indeed, requires a considerable degree of Christian maturity if it is to be met with proper composure.

Then there are the uncertainties and obscurities which at times accompany spiritual development in general. As an example consider the practice of prayer. Periodically there can be dryness, or a seeming inability to encounter God, and even a certain repugnance for the very exercise of prayer—these and other trials can be present, and we have the bothersome uncertainty which makes us wonder whether our prayer is proper, or even if it is prayer at all.

There can be a darkening of faith, and even a real crisis of faith; the uncertainty surrounding this trial can only be fully appreciated by those who have actually experienced it. Such a person, because of the psychological phenomena attached to this experience, can doubt whether he really believes any longer, although in reality he actually may be a firm believer.

There can also be the various uncertainties which surround the seemingly contradictory manifestations of God's will. There is a certain indication that God

would have us act this way, yet His will as channeled
to us from a different perspective seems to suggest another course of action. As a result we are somewhat
confused; we are uncertain, or at least we would prefer
a greater certitude, as to what God is asking of us.
These are a few examples of various types of uncertainty we can encounter in the following of Christ.
They are the kind which could confront a Christian
living in any age of the Church.

Today's Christian, however, lives in an age of accentuated uncertainty. In our previous chapter, we made
brief mention of this uncertainty which is accompanying life in a changing Church, an idea which will here
be developed more fully. The contemporary Church
renewal is laying bare every aspect of the Church's
life. It is fairly safe to say that there is no significant
dimension of the contemporary Church which has not
been opened up to the rethinking which has accompanied the Second Vatican Council. In the wake of this
surging renewal, various types of uncertainties have
rather suddenly thrust themselves into the lives of many
of the People of God. In various degrees these Christians have felt the pain which is a part of any type
of uncertainty.

The uncertainties which have risen in today's Church
are numerous. There is the uncertainty which accompanies doing things in a new way—and the Church is
doing a number of things in new ways on the universal,
national, diocesan, and parish levels. No one is exactly
certain what will emanate from these different ways
of doing old things and the completely new ways of
doing things which perhaps were never done before
in the history of the Church. That all this is causing
uncertainty in the minds of many of the Church's mem-

bers is apparent from such questions that one often hears these days: "Where is it all leading?" "What will the Church be like in ten years?"

To become more specific, there are uncertainties in today's Church which have arisen because of the external changes in the structure of the Church's life. To consider just one element of structural change, that of the liturgy, is enough to convince ourselves that change in structure does bring along with it a degree of uncertainty and confusion. Even many of those who are sincere, open to liturgical change, and optimistic about the new liturgy, have had their doubts and uncertainties as to what is authentic liturgy and authentic liturgical participation.

Another type of uncertainty which faces the members of the People of God today is that connected with the previously discussed diversification in the contemporary Church. The pre-Vatican II Church was a much more uniform Church than is today's. Then all more or less thought and acted in the same way. In the present-day Church, however, there is a newly discovered spirit of freedom and collegiality which has given rise to a pluralism of opinion and life-style. Insofar as the diverse ways contained in this pluralism are really inspired and guided by the Holy Spirit, we have a richer, more vital, and more attractive life within the Church. At the same time this increased diversification of the contemporary Church offers uncertainties that were not with us ten years ago. Just which theologians are correct on this or that point? Is it the conservative or liberal camp which is correct on this or that particular issue? These and similar questions are very much with us today, and they can cause a confusion and uncertainty which goes very deeply at times.

Closely connected with the decreased and changing structure in the Church, and also with the greater diversification just mentioned, is what is termed the new morality. It is not really a new morality. A better term would be a renewed morality, one which has achieved a renewed consciousness that the Christian life is radically rooted in the teaching of Scripture, especially the teaching of the Gospel.

This renewed morality is more interior, more consciously rooted in the Christian's personal freedom, initiative, and responsibility as enlightened by the interior law of grace, by the interior workings of the Holy Spirit. The new morality is a more satisfying one. Yet to say that it is more satisfying is not to say that it is an easier morality. If it respects the Christian's God-given freedom to a greater extent than the morality of by-gone days, it also demands more of his capacity for responsibility. The official teaching Church and her theologians are not spelling out in as great detail as formerly the practice of the Christian life. Taking just one example, we see this in the area of penance. The Church has all but done away with obligatory fast and abstinence on certain days. The Church is not telling us she no longer wishes us to practice penance and self-discipline. She rather is telling us that she thinks we are responsible enough to see this need in our lives and to practice it according to our own initiative. Moral theologians for their part have departed considerably from the overemphasis they once gave to casuistry—the endless list of solutions to particular moral cases or situations—and now are emphasizing more the general principles of morality.

This new morality, then, is not as minutely worked out by the official Church and theologians as was the case with the more traditional morality. Considerably more is being left to the individual Christian's personal freedom and responsibility. This morality, while being more authentic, also gives rise to more uncertainties. (Of course, in matters involving possible sin, we still must avoid acting in doubt. But our prudent certitude may not always be arrived at in the same manner as in the past.) These uncertainties are a necessary consequence of the fact that we now do not always have the hierarchical Church together with the theologians determining moral matters as specifically as in the past.

In summing up what we have said to this point, we can certainly state that the contemporary Christian is living in an age which has more than its share of uncertainty.

How should we act in times of uncertainty? The two great realities we have to be conscious of are those of love and trust. First, we must try to be particularly conscious of how much God loves us in Christ. This deepened realization, in turn, will lead us to a return of love, a love characterized by an abandoning trust in God's providence for us. Consequently, times of uncertainty can be times of tremendous growth, for we are creatures who can become too self-sufficient before God. We are prone to forget just how weak we are and how helpless we are without God. The discomfort of uncertainty can help arouse us from this false sense of security, for in such periods we are led to be more aware of our own helplessness, and we approach God for guidance, consolation and strength.

When we experience uncertainty we should also be aware of the fact that, although we do not possess all the light we would desire concerning the situation, we still can have that degree of enlightenment which God intends us to have. Furthermore, the general pattern of Christ's life is always before us as an example, and can be lived out in circumstances of uncertainty as well as at any other time. We can also utilize particular means which will possibly lessen or even dispel the uncertainty, or which will at least allow us to cope properly with the situation. Examples of such means are prayer, the seeking of advice from competent persons, and the reading of theological or other material pertinent to our difficulty or uncertainty.

We can also be helped during the times when uncertainty enters our lives if we realize that we come out of a spiritual tradition which has always had to face various kinds of uncertainty. In Old Testament times Abraham is an excellent example of this: "Yahweh said to Abram, 'Leave your country, your family and your father's house, for the land I will show you'." (Gen 12:1). If we reflect a few moments on these words, we begin to appreciate all the future uncertainties Abraham had to be willing to face if he wished to answer Yahweh's call. And he courageously did answer that call. In New Testament times we find the example of Mary and Joseph facing the uncertainties of the flight into Egypt.

Throughout the history of the Church one can easily observe that this biblical tradition of facing uncertainty has been admirably continued in so many instances and in so many ways. The history of the missionary effort of the Church is an example which readily comes to mind. In the lives of the great missionaries we read of their heroic virtue in facing innumerable difficulties and hardships, not least of which was not knowing what would confront them in strange lands and cultures populated by people so different from themselves, people who sometimes were deeply hostile.

The great founders of religious orders—both men and women—offer prime examples of Christians who were willing to live from day to day facing the great uncertainties of the task providence had placed before them. To build a religious family from nothing, to extend its apostolate over entire dioceses and nations, and even over the entire world—do we realize the enormous courage this demanded of religious founders and foundresses? They must have had to face many dark days filled with so many unknowns. Yet they did not falter. Although the path before them seemed so ill-lighted, or not lighted at all, they took a step at a time, and they never turned back. They trusted, and they trusted mightily, for if God called who were they to say the appointed task could not be accomplished? Precisely because these men and women were great in trust they were also great in accomplishment. A parallel case to founders of religious orders and congregations are those lay men and women who have started various lay movements. Two such members of the laity are Frederick Ozanam, the founder of the St. Vincent de Paul Society, and in our own times, the wonderful Dorothy Day. To meet Dorothy Day and discuss with her the work she founded and has continued must be a wonderful lesson in what it means to follow God's lead and trust utterly in Him although we cannot at all be sure where He is leading or what will happen.

In the same vein, though often unobserved and unsung, yet magnificent in example, are untold numbers of Christian parents down through the ages. In the face of nearly continuous uncertainties devolving upon them in the course of rearing their children—painful uncertainties of discipline and care—these parents have spent themselves with unfaltering trust in God. In accepting the tremendous responsibility of Christian parenthood, they have also accepted all its difficulties and uncertainties, and have often shown a devoted perseverance and an unfailing trust in God's continuing help. The countless numbers of sincere Christians in all walks of life throughout the ages has attested to the success of their parents' efforts.

There are also those innumerable people—bishops, priests, religious, laity—who have started and built up dioceses and parishes the world over. They are a hidden part of this spiritual tradition we are discussing, a tradition which we began with the example of Abraham and which has continued throughout the history of the Church, a tradition which has faced and conquered uncertainty of so many kinds.

We who live in these contemporary times of the post-Vatican II Church have a splendid opportunity of continuing the venturesome spirit we have been describing. As we mentioned before, in certain ways we do not feel as secure in today's Church as we did in the pre-Vatican II Church. The period of great religious transition in which we find ourselves is unmistakably a time of accentuated uncertainty of many kinds and degrees. But we all must realize that God in His providence has placed us in this time of the Church's history for a purpose. He wants us to meet the challenge of religious transition with courage, realism, initiative, and ingenuity. Although we cannot clearly detect where the Spirit is leading us, we have sufficient light to continue the journey. If we meet the challenge and continue to follow the authentic lead of the Spirit, we will be helping to shape a Church more capable of serving modern man. Despite the many unknown quantities which comprise this task God has put before the present-day Church, why should we fear, why should we hesitate? God loves us, and He loves us mightily, and He will never forget or abandon His people: "Does a woman forget her baby at the breast, or fail to cherish the son of her womb? Yet even if these forget, I will never forget you." (Is 49:15).

5

Dimensions
of Christian Love

All of us want to be great. We want to be persons of real significance. Perhaps we think such a desire is egotistic and unbecoming a Christian. However, this is simply not true if our desires for greatness are actually authentic. The example of the saints tells us this. They too wanted to be great. When told she was a nobody, St. Madeleine Sophie Barat determined that she would at least be great in humility. St. Therese of Lisieux, realizing that she could not accomplish the great mortifications of some of the saints, determined that she would be great in love in even the smallest matters. The saints are like the rest of mankind in desiring greatness. But, following the lead of Jesus, they know where to seek true greatness.

Christ in His own manner of life has vividly pointed out to all of us where true greatness lies. He tells us to seek greatness, but not to be deceived as to what it really is. Christ dealt with the powerful and the wealthy in His earthly existence, but He was not awed by them. As God He is, of course, infinitely greater than they, but even as man Christ realized He far surpassed them.

He knew that the Father had made His humanity perfect with the fullness of grace. Christ chose not to
surround this greatness with any trappings. Born into
this world in poverty and simplicity, looked down upon
as a Nazarene of no social status whatsoever, Christ
stands out as a giant of greatness. A man can possess
true greatness along with riches and social status, but
he is great not because of these. He is great because
of the manner in which he uses his riches and social
status. Christ tells us this. He tells us that a man is
great, not because of what he possesses, not because
of social status, not because he is admired by the
crowds, not even primarily because of great works he
might accomplish, but simply because of what he *is*.
For great works, if they really are authentically great,
are possible because of the innate greatness of the man
who achieves them. They are an incarnation, an exter-
nalization, of the primary greatness which is the man
himself.

Christ's greatness as man, then, was the innate greatness of His humanity itself. His greatness was the fullness and perfection of a truly human life, a life elevated
above its mere naturalness to a new dynamism, the life
of grace. Christ as man possessed this life of grace in
its fullness as a result of His human nature's close
union with the divine person of the Word. But Christ's
greatness was not an isolated greatness, an "unrelated"
greatness. It was rather a greatness which centered in
relationships of love.

Jesus' life was a life of love. He mightily loved His
Father and His fellow men. The greatness of Christ's
life can be comprehended only in terms of love, the
love which united Him so intimately to His Father and
to us. The poverty, the hiddenness, the disappoint-

ments, the accomplishments, the weariness, the joy and the happiness, the pain and the agony—all that comprised the earthly life of Christ was experienced and lived out within the framework of love. Jesus was the great man He was because He was a great lover. He loved in everything He did. He loved tenderly, manfully, with understanding and sympathy. He loved with complete devotedness and with a deep, sincere concern for the individual. He loved with a passion for that which was right and true and beautiful and good. He loved with a complete conformity to His Father's will. He loved always and completely. He loved with a gift of Himself, always pouring Himself out, even to the point of death. He gave Himself in love to the Father and to us until there was no more to give. This was the poignant beauty of Christ's life. This was His greatness. His greatness was centered in love. He was a giant of greatness because of what He simply *was*—a tremendous lover.

We can all say that at times we have not followed this marvelous example of Christ nearly as well as we could have. Too often we have sought our greatness and fulfillment in a manner which necessarily resulted sooner or later in disappointment. We have striven after greatness in ways God has not intended, and, consequently, as we reached out for our self-determined bubbles of achievement and fulfillment, these have burst at the touch. There has resulted a basic feeling of dissatisfaction, a kind of frustration, a realization that we were using the wrong key to life's meaning despite all the apparent promises that pointed to greatness and fulfillment. These promises have proven themselves false because they were not rooted in Christ and His way of life, His way to true personal greatness.

We must incessantly remind ourselves of the example Jesus has given us. We must deepen our realization that our fundamental greatness consists primarily in what we *are*. But if we are great because of what we *are*, we must always remember that we *are* to the extent that we love God and others. St. Paul in his own inimitable way tells us this: "If I have all the eloquence of men or of angels, but speak without love, I am simply a gong booming or a cymbal clashing. If I have the gift of prophecy, understanding all the mysteries there are, and knowing everything, and if I have faith in all its fulness, to move mountains, but without love, then I am nothing at all. If I give away all that I possess, piece by piece, and if I even let them take my body to burn it, but am without love, it will do me no good whatever." (1 Co 13:1-3).

Our greatness lies in our relating in love to God and men—yes, even to those whom we will never know or see directly, but whom nevertheless our love can reach out and touch because of our union with Christ. With Christ there are no space barriers, and therefore our love united to His can unite us to people the world over. Just as the Christ Who walked this earth was great because of what He *was*, a tremendous lover Who loved and opened Himself to being loved, so likewise we are great and achieve fulfillment to the degree that we love God and others and—very importantly—open ourselves up to His and their love.

We become authentic persons through a life centered in love, and within the milieu of the human condition. This is the only framework we have for achieving our greatness or true personhood. We must not shirk the human condition. Christ did not shirk it, but rather accepted the human condition and manifested His greatness within it, despite the pain and even agony this human condition at times heaped upon Him. It is true that Jesus was buoyed up during the course of His life by the goodness, sincerity and response of some of those to whom He preached. And the love which Mary and Joseph gave Him is incomprehensible. But often during His life Jesus suffered because of the evil side of men—their pettiness, cowardice, insensitivity, self-ishness, meanness, and egotism. This suffering because of the limitations of others began at Christ's very birth. Mary had to bring Jesus into this world amid such poor and uncomfortable circumstances because the people of Bethlehem did not measure up to the situation. They were not the persons they should have been. As Joseph sought shelter for himself and his lovely Mary, it was obvious to those he encountered that his wife was with child. Despite the crowded conditions in Bethlehem caused by the census-taking, surely some kind of decent dwelling could have been provided Joseph and Mary— and Jesus—if some of the townspeople had been gen-erous enough to arrange suitable shelter even at some cost to themselves. But they failed their opportunity, and Mary and Joseph and Jesus suffered because of their lack of response. Many, many times throughout Christ's life this incident would in some way be re-peated. He would suffer at the hands of others because they were not what they should have been. Yet these experiences did not thwart the greatness of Jesus. Christ always was what *He* should have been despite the limitations of the human condition which surrounded Him. He was always the tremendous lover, and He loved even at those times when it was very painful to do so.

Our own greatness in Christ, our growth in the

Christian life with its center of love, can develop smoothly and joyfully because of the goodness and love in the hearts of others. They make it easy for us to love as we should. But at other times the less wholesome side of men and the human condition crowds in upon us, and we find it so difficult to go on loving as we should. For as it was in Christ's life, we, too, as we exercise our Christian love, suffer because of others. We suffer because people are dull and insensitive. We suffer because others do not always understand us, no, not even those who love us dearly. We suffer because some are not appreciative of what we do for them, sometimes at a great personal cost. We suffer because others reject us, or because they make us the objects of their meanness and selfishness. We suffer because there are some who ignore us. Others can make us suffer in so many different ways, and at times we suffer so much that we are tempted to quit loving as we know we should. We are tempted to withdraw from the pain of giving oneself in love, to withdraw into an egotistic enclosure of self-seeking, where, we wrongly think, we will no longer suffer at the hands of others, or at least not as much. But to surrender to such a temptation is to forget what Christian greatness really is—a life of love of God and man, a love which does not shrink from the pain caused from loving in the human condition, a love which is meant to become greater and the more selfless precisely because of the limitations of those who surround us.

We have been developing a general framework of Christian love, the heart of the Christian life. Now let us consider in some detail the various specific dimensions of Christian love. These are four: our openness to God's love for us, our love for God, our love for man, and our openness to receiving love from others. These dimensions are distinct aspects of the Christian experience of love, yet they are intended by God to be intimately interwoven. As one progresses in the Christian life, all four dimensions become more and more profoundly united.

The first dimension of Christian love, our openness to God's love for us, is an extremely important one, because it gets right at the heart of the supernatural. Throughout salvation history God has always taken the initiative, loving us first. We are completely helpless in the supernatural order without God first communicating Himself. We cannot give the supernatural life to ourselves by our mere natural powers. It is only with God's totally free gift of grace, elevating our natural faculties, that we are initiated into this life and grow in it. Each gift of the Christian life is God loving us. The Incarnate Word Himself, Mary, the Church, the sacraments, the Eucharistic liturgy, Scripture, habitual and actual grace, and all the rest—these are God's gifts of love. He loves each of us through these gifts in a very personal, intimate, and unique way. True, these are gifts to the total community which is the People of God. But they are also gifts to us individually.

As we open ourselves to God's love, we approach ever closer to the fullness of the Christian life. Our problem is that we often shy away from God's love for us. Although we are fundamentally redeemed, we are not yet completely redeemed. There is still a sinful dimension within us which pulls against our basic orientation to God. We are afraid of what it will cost if we open ourselves completely to God's love. It seems to us that the white heat of His love is too overwhelming. We fear that if we are too much possessed by God that our lives will have to change. We feel that our freedom will be too much curtailed, that God will become more of a master of our lives than we wish. We feel that our quest for our kind of fulfillment will be thwarted. God's ways are not always our ways, and His ways—well, at times we would just as soon not follow them.

All this is a strange attitude to have toward God's love for us, is it not? Yet we all have to admit that this manner of thinking too much influences our existence. How erroneous this attitude is becomes obvious to us as we reflect in mature faith on the meaning of God's love. God's love for us in the Christian life is meant to bring us to a peace and happiness that we could otherwise not experience. God's love for us is not meant to subtract in any way from enjoying authentic human existence. Rather, as we open ourselves to this divine love, we live more vitally, we increasingly experience the true meaning of life, and we achieve a personal fulfillment that a way of life cut off from openness to God's love, or not expansively open to it, could never give us. It is for us, then, to grow in the realization of God's love for us, its meaning, and its depth. As St. Paul reminds us, if God loved us so much when we were His enemies, how much more He loves us now: "We were still helpless when at his appointed moment Christ died for sinful men. It is not easy to die even for a good man—though of course for someone really worthy, a man might be prepared to die—but what proves that God loves us is that Christ died for us while we were still sinners. Having died to make us righteous, is it likely that he would now fail to save us from God's anger?" (Rm 5:6-9).

Our response in love to God and His love for us constitutes a second dimension of Christian love. This

response must center in a loving conformity to the
Father's will. This is the example Christ has given us.
The new Dutch Catechism tells us: "To sum up Jesus'
personal 'spirituality' in one word, one would say simply: the will of God."[1] Scripture itself tells us that the
Father's will was the guiding principle of Jesus' life.
The Epistle to the Hebrews in speaking of Christ
states: ". . . and this is what he said, on coming into the
world: You who wanted no sacrifice or oblation, prepared a body for me. You took no pleasure in holo-
causts or sacrifices for sin: then I said, just as I was
commanded in the scroll of the book, 'God, here I am!
I am coming to obey your will.'" (Heb 10:5-7).

As Christ's life was supremely successful because He
perfectly loved His Father's will, likewise must the
life of each of us be judged—this life which is our response in love. At times we tend to judge the value of
our lives not by first looking to God's will, but rather by
primarily considering the external success of our work,
the fact that we are being loved and accepted by others,
or the fact that we are feeling particularly worthwhile.
Let us make ourselves very clearly understood here. We
are not saying that a person's existence which is here
and now characterized by the above cannot be one
deeply conformed in love to the Father's will, and,
therefore, a highly successful and valuable existence.
But this is not always the case. Sometimes our lives
could possess the above characteristics and yet not be
significantly guided by the divine will; and to the
extent that God's will is not permitted to influence our
lives, to that extent they lack real value, despite all the
appearances to the contrary.

[1] *A New Catechism* (New York: Herder & Herder, 1967), p. 123.

On the other hand, we can be tempted to think our lives are useless, or, even worse, a nuisance to ourselves and others because of the mere *appearance* of unsuccessful living. We may be presently feeling weighted down by a continued sense of frustration, or everyone seems to be failing to really understand us, or appreciate our work, or a particular trial seems to keep nagging at us—and the list could go on and on. During such periods we must resist the temptation to look upon our lives as unsuccessful. Even though the suffering may be cutting deep, and our lives seem to lack success and value, we must realize through reflective faith that our existence in the painful here and now is greatly worthwhile as long as we are reaching out to embrace the Father's will with love, yes, even though our love at the time may seem so weak, and frustrated, and almost shattered.

If in our vision of faith we are personally convinced that the success and worth of our existence is evaluated by the degree to which God's will possesses us, then we should be concerned to grow in a proper sensitivity to the Father's will. We should be aware that His will comes to us not only in the ten commandments and the commandments of the Church, but also in so many other ways. For instance, it comes to us through the pages of Scripture, through the needs of others, through the inspirations of grace, and through the various circumstances which divine providence at least permits to come into our lives. If we do become aware of the varied manner in which the Father manifests His will, and if we become increasingly convinced that our love for God has to assimilate this will, then our Christian love will continue to rest upon solid ground and not sand. We will be implementing the words of Jesus to us: "It is not those who say to me, 'Lord, Lord,' who will enter the kingdom of heaven, but the person who does the will of my Father in heaven." (Mt 7:21).

Much of God's will as regulating our Christian existence is concerned with directing our attention towards our neighbor. This concept leads us to a third dimension of Christian love, love of our fellowman. The great importance God places on love of neighbor is brought out in the words of our Lord: "Then the King will say to those on his right hand, 'Come, you whom my Father has blessed, take for your heritage the kingdom prepared for you since the foundation of the world. For I was hungry and you gave me food; I was thirsty and you gave me drink . . .' Then the virtuous will say to him in reply, 'Lord, when did we see you hungry and feed you; or thirsty and give you drink? . . .' And the King will answer, 'I tell you solemnly, in so far as you did this to one of the least of these brothers of mine, you did it to me.'" (Mt 25:34-40).

The contemporary Christian has a special responsibility and privilege as a bearer of love for one's brother. A Christian of any age certainly has a duty of love towards mankind, but our present day world has special need of people who love their brothers and love them deeply. This is so because of the critical times in which we live. The human race is faced with enormous problems, and many of these are caused because there is not enough love in the hearts of men. Not only is there not enough love, but in certain cases there is deep hatred. We do not want to look only at the darker side of today's world. As Christians who believe that Christ has victoriously redeemed the world, conquering even death itself in His resurrection, we should always be fundamentally optimistic. We should always be aware that Christ's redemption has let loose a torrent of grace which is meant to permeate mankind more and more. This Christic grace works not only in the hearts of professed Christians, but it works in the hearts of all men, in so many hidden ways, and so we have that great number of people whom contemporary theologians call nameless or anonymous Christians. They are so named because they can, unaware to themselves, be responding to Christic grace. This Christic grace, working in Christian and non-Christian alike, is at work to make us persons who love God and man. This Christic grace has accomplished marvels of love. The examples of love for one's brothers are being multiplied countlessly each day the world over. Because good can be so hidden, and because it does not usually make headlines, we can be unaware of the vast good which does exist in men's hearts.

But there is a darker side. War is still with us. Great poverty, with its concomitant scourge of disease, mars too much of the face of the earth. Much of this poverty is caused by the selfishness in the hearts of some, a selfishness which manifests a callous lack of love for one's neighbor. In our own United States we have enormous social problems. We have a gigantic racial problem. We have peddlers of drugs and pornographic literature who are selfishly becoming rich off the physical and moral ruin of those to whom they cater. These are examples of some of the decay which eats away at our society. And why do we have these problems? One chief reason is that in one way or the other men have failed to love their brothers as they should. As our gaze sweeps over our own America and the rest of the world, and we see what happens when man fails to love his neighbor, we have to be aware of the special danger this lack of love carries for our contemporary age. We live in an atomic age. If modern man would continue too much on a path of lack of love and concern for his brother, the result could be tragic. Modern man has the power to destroy himself. He must learn to grow more and more in love for his neighbor if this threat is to become less and less a possibility.

We repeat—we contemporary Christians have a special obligation to give a witness as to what it means to love one's brother. Not only can we be an external example of love, but every time we love our neighbor we are also adding a bit to that vibrant force of world-love, a force which can be increasingly powerful to change further the face of the earth. Very importantly also, the more selflessly we Christians love one another and mankind the world over through the tangibleness of our humanity, the more we help to continue one of the great laws of the Incarnation. Through the human enfleshment of Jesus, God channeled His love to mankind in a visible, tangible, and human manner. The Church and each Christian are continuations of the Incarnation. United to the glorified Christ, we too are meant to be visible manifestations of God's love to men. We too are human instruments of His love.

There are various characteristics of an authentic Christian love for one's neighbor. Our love should be universal, excluding no one. Our love can reach out and touch men the world over through such means as prayer. If Christ's love included all men, so also must ours. Another characteristic of our love for mankind is that it should incarnate itself in some form of service. Christ came to serve. This must also be our desire. Any authentic occupation, if I approach it with the correct attitude, can be this service to mankind. A laborer, doctor, nurse, teacher, businessman, engineer—all of these can be persons rendering a service of love to man, or they can be persons primarily motivated by money or some other less worthy motive. It all depends on one's attitude. A third characteristic of our love for others, and this pertains to those whom we contact directly, is that it should possess a human warmth. Christ as man loved with His total humanity, emotions included. In the proper sense of the phrase, Christ was a deeply emotional man because He was gifted with a perfect set of emotions. He wept over Lazarus' grave and He wept over Jerusalem. He must have had a real human warmth, for the children loved to flock to Him, and we all know that children shy away from cold personalities. We also must allow a real human warmth to penetrate our love for others. The manner in which this displays itself must obviously respect the persons involved. We love friends in a way different from a man loving his wife, or parents their children. A final characteristic of our love for our neighbor is that it is willing to take the risk of loving without receiving love in return. Everyone desires to be recognized for service rendered. Everyone wants to receive love for love given. But the mature Christian will not demand such recompense. Hurt as it may, he will love even though he is not loved in return, or worse still, is even hated for his efforts. This is perhaps the most difficult lesson to learn concerning love for one's neighbor, but how important a lesson it is.

With certain of those whom we directly encounter we will form interpersonal relationships. The prime example is the encounter between man and woman which leads to marriage. But there are other kinds of interpersonal relationships, too. For instance, there is that between friends. There is that between parents and children, and between the children themselves. These interpersonal relationships can grow and become very deep and intimate and beautiful. They can be existential and vivid witness to the marvels which human love can achieve as aided by Christian grace. These interpersonal relationships are a reflection in space and time of the deep love relationships which unite the divine persons of the Trinity. They are fully intended by God, and both Church and world need more of these relationships which are really deep. Too few of these interpersonal relationships are really as deep and beautiful and intimate as they should be. This is so because there are too few really mature persons who sufficiently understand the meaning of love and are willing to pay the price which its full development and grandeur demand. Should not we Christians be leading the way?

We have discussed God's love for us, our love for God, and our love for neighbor. The final dimension of Christian love is one which seems to be too much neglected. It is openness in receiving love from others. Here again the type of relationship determines the manner in which the love is received. A man receives love from his wife differently than he does from his son or a friend. This dimension of Christian love is so important because it is necessary if the various mutual bonds of love uniting men are to be strengthened. Many can love others in a functional way, but they seem unable to really receive love from others in a Christian openness. They encounter the others—even their partners in marriage—on a superficial level, and in such cases there is usually very little real communication. There is too little real openness.

We began our treatment of Christian love by focusing our gaze on the Incarnation. We discussed the Incarnate Word, Jesus of Nazareth, as the tremendous lover. We conclude by again directing our attention to Christ. He came to teach us about love. He revealed to us how much God loves us. He told us how much we are to love God—with our whole being. He taught us how God wants us to love one another so deeply. To the extent that we have understood what Jesus came to teach about love, to that extent we understand the essence of Christianity. To the extent we live what we understand, to that extent we are mature Christians. In the words of St. Paul: "In short there are three things that last: faith, hope and love; and the greatest of these is love." (1 Co 13:13).

6

Supports to Love:
Other Christian Virtues

Christian love, which we have just considered according to various dimensions, is at the heart of our Christian life. Our life of grace, which is a participation in God's Trinitarian life, expresses itself primarily through love. Yet Christian love cannot stand alone. There are other Christian virtues which serve as aids to love. These virtues help remove the obstacles which prevent a proper growth of Christian love. They also help channel love, for these virtues are attitudes or positive dispositions of the Christian which allow him to relate properly in love to God, man, and material creation.

Our present purpose does not allow for a treatment of all the Christian virtues, nor for a complete treatment of any of them. We will merely make certain observations concerning some of these virtues.

Faith

Christian faith accompanies love in a most special manner. These two comprise the most important virtues, for they, among all the virtues, assimilate us most intimately to God's life. God's life is a life of divine knowing and loving, and through Christian faith and love we participate in these Trinitarian operations.

There are special problems and obstacles which the modern Christian has to encounter in his life of faith. One of these is the fact that he does not live in an atmosphere of faith. Long ago in the golden age of Christendom there was this atmosphere. Practically everybody with whom one lived and worked was a believer. Today we find ourselves at the opposite end of the gamut. One experiences various forms of disbelief not only in the world at large, but in some cases within one's own family, or among those with whom one has shared the mystery of Christ within the Christian community. Rahner puts it in this manner: "A Christian's faith is not a purely private concern. We live in the community of faith which is called the Church, but in practice we are a 'diaspora' everywhere today, sometimes even among our own relatives. I do not refer to ecclesiastical divisions, to the fact that various Christian bodies are represented in our environment and even among our relatives; I mean that quite a number of people in our environment—let us face it—have in effect lost the faith, some of them becoming real enemies to the Church and officially leaving her."[1]

Another faith problem facing the contemporary Christian is the doctrinal situation within the Church. Concomitant with the deep-rooted change in today's Church there has arisen a certain theological and doctrinal confusion. All things considered, this has perhaps been inevitable. The teaching of the Church is to a certain

[1] Karl Rahner, *Do you Believe in God?* (New York: Newman Press, 1969), p. 19.

extent being recast in language more relevant and meaningful for contemporary man. There are also theological speculations among professional theologians, which,
when reflected through the prism of the mass media, sometimes become distorted and cause considerable confusion among the faithful. And to be perfectly
honest, we have to admit that, along with much good
theology, there has been some bad and unsound theology making the rounds in the post-Vatican II Church.
All of these factors have contributed to a confused situation which does not make the life of faith any easier.

But whatever the problems confronting the man of
faith in this or any age may be, we do know that God's
grace compensates for these problems and difficulties.
If the faith of today's Christian is being especially put
to the test, God is also giving special graces that Christian faith may be preserved and developed.

What does faith accomplish in us? The contemporary
theology of faith emphasizes that faith establishes a
personal relationship between the Christian and God in
Christ. Faith is concerned primarily with a response to
the personal God, and only secondarily, but definitely
very importantly, with the truths God reveals. This
should not surprise us, for there is a similarity as regards
our relationships with human persons. A person of low
character and known to be a liar does not elicit our
trust. Whatever he says, we tend to disbelieve. On the
other hand, we tend to believe whatever a person of
good character tells us. Human faith, then, directs us
first to the person, and then to what he says. Divine
faith acts similarly. It directs us primarily to God Himself, and secondarily to the truths He gives us. But
faith not only establishes a special personal relationship
between the believer and man. Because of the new

vision of his neighbor which faith gives to the believer, it calls him to a faith-inspired relationship with the neighbor. Faith is truly person orientated—directing the believer to God and man, and formative of personal relationships accordingly.

Faith involves not only the intellect. It is meant to involve the entire man. This is the biblical concept of faith. True, the graced intellect assents to the truths God reveals, but one's whole being is also meant to assent. Christian faith ideally is the commitment of the complete Christian to God in Christ. Mature faith is the complete dedication of oneself and all of one's powers and capacities to Jesus and to His cause.

Because faith is the commitment of one's entire being to the truth of Jesus, we must live the truth of Jesus, not merely intellectually assent to it, if we are to assimilate Christ's revelation properly. Religious truth is comprehended as it should be only when we live it, savor it, experience it, to the depths of our being. We have all experienced this. How much more we have understood the truth of Christ and its power and wisdom and beauty when we were not only assenting to this truth with our intellects, but were also living it, allowing it to permeate and transform our entire existence. As a corollary of this, we see the danger of intellectually assenting to Christ's truth without attempting to live accordingly. One's faith can grow weak and even die when there is a constant and serious dichotomy between what we belive and the manner in which we live.

If we grow in faith by ourselves living its truth, we also progress faith-wise by witnessing the truth of Christ in the lives of others. This is an application of the principle of continued Incarnation. In the historical

Incarnation Jesus taught us the truth of the Father not only verbally, but also by His own living of that truth. God intends this process to continue. God hands on the truth of Christ not only through various verbal forms such as the official teaching of the Church, but also in part by the manner in which Christians live this truth. One reason Christianity has not had a greater influence in the world is the fact that it is only in a relatively small number of Christian lives that the truth of Christ has been properly assimilated and manifested; and the truth of Christ tends to have its full attractive force both for those within and outside the Church only when it is seen to be lived out concretely by Christians who profess this truth. Our faith is blessed when we ourselves encounter such Christians.

When we live according to faith we are living according to a certain vision of God, of man, and material creation. Faith tells us things about God and creation that we could not otherwise know, or know only with greater difficulty and with less certainty. A good example of the former is the doctrine of the Trinity. Unaided reason could never arrive at this sublime truth. It is only the intellect which has been elevated with the grace of faith that can encounter the Triune God.

If we are to progress properly in the Christian life we must allow the vision of faith to penetrate our activity more and more. We should become increasingly contemplatives in action. We should see everything as God sees it. And everything we see should increasingly remind us of God, for everything which is good and true and beautiful does really reflect God. The raging storm at sea reflects the power of God, and the beauties of nature manifest His beauty. The stillness of the forest reminds us of the holy silence of God.

The goodness, the kindness, and the love we see in human persons tell us that God is infinitely good and kind and loving.

The vision of faith allows us to see man and his world in a manner far different from that of the non-believer. As contemplatives in action we should act upon this vision. Every man, woman, and child is marked with the blood of Christ. If Jesus loved them so much, if He now loves them so much, can we be indifferent to their needs, both spiritual and material? Can we be indifferent to all the contemporary problems which weigh modern man? If we are Christians of living faith we know that we cannot be indifferent. The vision of faith should inspire us to action according to our vocation, talents, opportunity, time and energy. We should be laboring to make man and his world more Christic. To the extent that we do not, we are betraying the vision of faith.

Hope

Christian hope is a virtue which allows us to tend toward God in Christ as our absolute fulfillment, as our absolute future. Hope also allows us to trust that God will grant us the graces necessary to achieve this goal which is Himself.

The necessity of hope in our lives is obvious. Without a sustained desire for God as our absolute future we will not live as we should. If God is not our goal then our lives will be miserably shaped by something infinitely less—whether it be money, sex, social status, or anything else which can often grip men's hearts as an unauthentic end rather than as a legitimate means to God as our absolute future. The necessity of hope

is also realized as we examine the nature of the supernatural. Without God's grace we cannot initially attain
the supernatural life, we cannot maintain ourselves in
it, we cannot grow in it. At times God allows us to
experience very strikingly and very deeply how helpless
we are without Him. Such episodes in the spiritual
journey can be very painful, but they can also be opportunities for great growth. We are meant to emerge from
this kind of experience with an increase of trust in God,
realizing how weak we are in ourselves, but how strong
we are if we rely on Him. Let us remember also that as
we trust in God so shall we receive. There are certainly
exceptions to this rule, and God can give great graces
to a person at a time when his trust is feeble—but the
general principle stands. In our Christian hope let us
expect great things from God—remembering what truly
great things are in the sight of God—and not only for
ourselves but for others, too. The fact that our hope
should be directed towards the needs of others as well
as our own leads us to another dimension of hope.

Hope is not only personal—directed at one's self—
it is also ecclesial. We are members of the Body of
Christ, the People of God, and we go to the Father in
Christ and by the Spirit not as isolated individuals but
as members of a community. Consequently, our hope
should be concerned with the total progress of the
Church. The Church is meant to assimilate Christ more
and more, for she is a pilgrim Church and she will not
have arrived at her final growth in Christ until the end
of time. Meanwhile our Christian hope should inspire
us to labor that the imperfections and sinfulness of the
Church decrease, as her people reach out in hope for a
greater participation in realized eschatology, a greater
sharing here and now in that which will be fully possessed only in eternity.

Christian hope, while being personal and ecclesial, is also cosmic. We hope that not only ourselves and the entire People of God will be assimilated to Christ more intimately now and finally possess Him in eternity. We hope that mankind in general and the whole of creation evolve closer to their omega point Who is Christ. St. Paul reminds us of this cosmic dimension of Christian hope: "The whole creation is eagerly waiting for God to reveal his sons. It was not for any fault on the part of creation that it was made unable to attain its purpose, it was made so by God; but creation still retains the hope of being freed, like us, from its slavery to decadence, to enjoy the same freedom and glory as the children of God. From the beginning till now the entire creation, as we know, has been groaning in one great act of giving birth; and not only creation, but all of us who possess the first-fruits of the Spirit, we too groan inwardly as we wait for our bodies to be set free." (Rm 8:19-23).

In summary, we hope for ourselves, for the entire People of God, for all men and all creation. Christian hope is personal, ecclesial, and cosmic. In each instance, if our hope is really authentic, we pledge ourselves to take the necessary means to achieve what we are hoping for. We commit ourselves to this necessary labor here and now, for the day will come for each of us when time will be no more: "As long as the day lasts I must carry out the work of the one who sent me; the night will be here when no one can work." (Jn 9:4).

Realizing Our Creaturehood

Humility, or realizing one's status as God's creature, is not too much spoken about or written of today, but its perennial importance is accentuated by Jesus Himself: "Shoulder my yoke and learn from me, for I am gentle and humble in heart, and you will find rest for your souls." (Mt 11:29). Jesus as man was perfectly humble. He realized that His humanity was a gift from God. All the perfections of that humanity, both natural and supernatural, were gifts of God. Jesus as man, realizing His creaturehood, was perfectly submissive to the divine will. He was perfectly humble.

Humility, then, is truth. It is man's realization of his creaturehood. It is the realization that all of one's endowments are ultimately gifts of God. Humility is also the realization that as a creature I have an obligation to use and develop these gifts according to God's design. Humility bids the Christian to allow God to direct his life. We have a tendency sometimes not to realize sufficiently these truths. We are tempted to usurp some of God's dominion and tend to attribute our gifts to ourselves. We have to be careful not to become like the Gospel Pharisee: "He spoke the following parable to some people who prided themselves on being virtuous and despised everyone else, 'Two men went up to the Temple to pray, one a Pharisee, the other a tax collector. The Pharisee stood there and said this prayer to himself, "I thank you, God, that I am not grasping, unjust, adulterous like this tax collector here. I fast twice a week; I pay tithes on all I get." The tax collector stood some distance away, not daring even to raise his eyes to heaven; but he beat his breast and said, "God, be merciful to me, a sinner." This man, I tell you, went home again at rights with God; the other did not. For everyone who exalts himself will be humbled, but the man who humbles himself will be exalted.'" (Lk 18: 9-14).

The Pharisee in this parable is a prime example of self-righteousness. He is a self-made saint, and, therefore, in God's eyes is no saint at all. He looks upon himself as the perfect model of what a religious man should be, and thinks that he himself should receive the glory and praise for what he thinks he has accomplished. He does not ask God for anything, because he is not aware of needing anything. To him religion is the proper type of external conformity and he can attend to this himself. The publican, on the other hand, realizes his own nothingness. He realizes that this is what he must bring to God—his nothingness—and that if he does God will fill him with *His* righteousness, *His* justification, *His* grace. The publican in his humility is open to God's self-communication, and he is the type who would always recognize the source of his religious gifts—God Himself.

Humility, because it is truth, does not prevent us from acknowledging our gifts of nature and grace; it merely bids us to recognize God as the source of these gifts. Actually, we should not try to deny our gifts. If we do not recognize them we will not properly thank God for what He has given us, and we will fail to develop these talents as we should.

The contemporary world is so much in need of the spirit of humility. We are not denying the basic goodness of the world, the fact that there is so much goodness in so many human hearts. But honesty demands that we realistically admit to what is wrong with the world. While affirming the goodness of the world, we have to hate what is evil. Part of the evil of today's world is the fact that there is so much of the spirit of self-sufficiency. So many men consider themselves complete masters of their own destiny and so capable of shaping the destiny of others. God has no part in the picture. Whatever man has and achieves is entirely to the credit of man himself and no one else. If man is given enough time, he will cure all the basic problems of society and man will have arrived definitively at his own self-made fulfillment and happiness. This is the kind of thinking which dominates too much of the contemporary world. Christians will not change this spirit overnight. But their own exercise of humility, of the realization of their creaturehood, should be a thrust which helps to prevent the world from becoming in attitude completely self-sufficient, with no thought of its need of God. If that happened, we would have our brand of contemporary cosmic pharisaism—a world thinking it had no needs for which it could not itself provide.

Moderating the Pleasurable

The attitude of moderateness we are now going to discuss has been traditionally termed the virtue of Christian temperance. This attitude allows us to relate properly to the pleasurable in life. God has filled our world with all sorts of good things and has given us the capacity to enjoy these. He wants us to enjoy the pleasurable, but He wants us to do so according to His will.

Without an attitude of temperance one's life would become soft and selfish, given over too much to the pursuit of pleasure, a life bent on self-satisfaction rather than properly directed to the loving service of God and man. Because of the intense attractive power of that which is pleasurable, man indeed can quickly become less than human without the control of temperance.

But there is an aspect of temperance or moderation that is often overlooked. The temperate person enjoys the pleasurable more than does one who is intemperate. The intemperate person is one who is a slave to his desires. His desires, to the degree that they are inordinate, are cut off from the rational control of the intellect and will. In this state these desires become insatiable and can never be satisfied, and the man who gives in to them is ultimately enjoying the pleasurable less. As the cigarette advertisement would have it, "Are you smoking more and enjoying it less? Switch to _____ cigarettes." In our context, if a person is seeking more and more pleasure and enjoying it less and less, he should be advised to switch to temperance. Grace does not destroy nature but brings it to perfection, to a fulfillment it could not otherwise attain. Our God-given capacity to enjoy the pleasurable actually is enhanced by the virtue of moderation. Temperance bids us to regulate the pleasurable, and even at times to renounce the pleasurable if this is necessary to achieve the proper control. All this contains its own kind of pain and effort, but an effort which leads to a deepened enjoyment of that to which God has attached pleasure.

The attitude of moderation is particularly necessary for us who live in an affluent society. We have at our disposal many forms of pleasure and recreation. With the trend toward a shorter work week we will increasingly have time to enjoy these. The Christian in this day and age, consequently, is being given a particular opportunity to develop a theology of play and leisure. A sense of Christian temperance or moderation will help him to develop this theology authentically. It will help him to integrate properly the theology of play and leisure with the theology of work and service.

Facing the Difficult

Human nature has a very obvious tendency to try to avoid that which is hard, difficult, arduous. Perhaps one of the most common obstacles to continued progress in the spiritual life is lack of constancy in striving for the difficult Gospel ideal. This failure on the part of some to endure the arduous in God's service is nothing new. In Old Testament times, one of the great tasks of the prophets was to remind the Israelites of their serious sinfulness and to strive to bring them back to Yahweh's law. They had become disloyal because they were not willing to bear with that which was difficult and arduous in the life of the covenant. This same problem has remained in various degrees throughout the history of the new convenant, the Church. Part of the Church's history is the failure of some Christians of all vocations to face courageously the arduous in Christ's service.

The need for a Christian virtue which enables us successfully to encounter the difficult is therefore obvious. Traditionally this virtue has been called fortitude. Today we may prefer another name, such as strength of heart or courage. Whatever name we give it, it is the essence of this virtue which is ultimately important.

All members of the People of God, regardless of their vocation, are constantly in need of this virtue. The insistent demands made upon the married are numberless. To be a committed Christian husband and father or wife and mother, demands a courage and strength of heart which borders on the heroic when exercised properly over the years. This is particularly true when physical or spiritual misfortune make tragic entrance into family life and leave in their wake deep bewilderment and heartache. For instance, who but those who have actually experienced it, can realize the crushing sorrow which attacks a conscientious father and mother when one of their children turns out to be a moral degenerate? Despite their constant efforts to rear their children according to Christian principles, this has happened. A high degree of Christian courage is demanded to cope properly with such situations.

The priestly and religious states of life also offer daily and numerous occasions for the exercise of Christian fortitude. This is especially true today when a significant number of priests and religious are searching for their identity in the contemporary Church. An added burden to the problems and difficulties which priests and religious encounter in their service to the People of God and the rest of mankind is the fact that the difficult and arduous must be shouldered within the framework of a celibate life. The joy, happiness, warmth, and support of marriage and family life are not present for the priest and religious to lighten the difficulties of their vocations. This is not said to argue against the celibate state, for it has its own particular support and consolation. But it takes a special grace-given strength of heart to bear with the deprivations of the celibate state and to develop its positive values, thus assuring that the one living priestly or religious celibacy makes his proper and joyous contribution to the life of the Church.

There are also difficulties common to all states of life. The Christian life obviously is essentially the same for all. It is arduous for a Christian to pray consistently whether he be priest, religious, or layman. To bear with the monotonous element of daily life without allowing it to stamp out the enthusiasm we should have in Christ's service is another common difficulty we all encounter. Fidelity to work and duty even when it seems to go unnoticed and unappreciated—who of us has not realized the courage this demands?

The above are a few examples of the difficult in God's service which could be experienced in any age of

Christianity. Today, as we all are aware, we live in especially difficult times as regards both the Church and human society at large. To live in a changing Church amid its process of deep-rooted change is a difficult task no matter how optimistic we may be about the outcome. Not to shy away from our part in the renewal process, to maintain a sense of balance amid a certain amount of confusion which has accompanied change and renewal, to try to remain open and united in love with those who think and act differently than we do in the contemporary Church—all this requires an uncommon degree of courageous dedication. Added to the demands made on our fortitude in today's Church is the fact that this Church is situated in a fast-paced, rapidly changing world with all the problems and difficulties springing forth from such a society. The crucial and difficult issues facing modern man are staggering, and the Christian should bear his part of the burden. He should even be taking the initiative. Here again the demand for courage and constancy in the face of the difficult is incessant. In conclusion we can say without being guilty of an overstatement: the arduous and difficult arising out of one's basic Christian vocation today, out of the duties of his state in life, and out of his contemporary Church and world, make the virtue of Christian courage or fortitude not the least necessary for successful living in the present age.

Giving Others Their Due

The virtue which has traditionally been called justice bids us to give to others what is their due. We must respect the life, good name, and the property of another. We owe this to others because they have rights con-

cerning these values. Also, whatever our work or profession may be, we must give our diligent and reasonable best to our employer and to those others whom we
serve through our labor. These truths seem to be fairly
evident to any sincere Christian.

However, in the area of social justice there does not
seem to be the same proportionate awareness. The
action of the People of God concerning the implementation of the principles of social justice does not consti-
tute a very stellar performance. It is not that we lack
theory. In our times the theory of social justice has been
brilliantly given through the five great papal encyclicals dealing with social issues and problems. This list
of encyclicals is comprised of Leo XIII's *Rerum No-
varum,* Pius XI's *Quadragesimo Anno,* John XXIII's
Mater et Magistra and *Pacem in Terris,* and Paul VI's
Progressio Populorum.

Time may be running out. The seething social problems in the United States alone are constantly breaking
forth into various types of violence. The very survival
of our nation as we have known it may depend on how
quickly and how effectively we address ourselves to
the solution of our social ills. As we turn our gaze
around the world we see more of the same.

The problem must be attacked through individual
and collective effort in every reasonable way. In whatever manner the Christian's profession or work offers
an opportunity to promote social justice, such an occasion must be used to the utmost. As far as vocation,
time, and energy allow, Christians should devote themselves to civic or Church organizations designed for the
prevention and cure of social ills. Christianity has had
its great social apostles in the past. We have them now,
but they are too few in number. We need more. We

have to make up for lost time. "For I was hungry and you gave me food; I was thirsty and you gave me drink; I was a stranger and you made me welcome; naked and you clothed me. . . ." (Mt 25:35-36).

Making Christianity Attractive

Human nature, in the very depths of its reality as created by God, is drawn to the good, the beautiful, and the attractive, and is repelled by that which is evil and unattractive. This basic truth cannot be denied, although in some instances man's perception of what is good or attractive may be distorted. In his needs and desires, in his wishes and hopes, man is constantly tending toward that which he perceives as good.

Human nature in its entirety has been elevated to a new level of existence in Christ. Man's desire for the good, the beautiful, the attractive, now has a deepened and Christic orientation. Man tends toward Jesus as total goodness. We Christians have a special role in the movement of man towards Jesus as the source of good. In the Scriptures Jesus Himself acknowledged His need and desire to have us assist Him in the promulgation of the Gospel: "Go, therefore, make disciples of all the nations . . ." (Mt 28:19). Through these words the Christian has been commissioned to attempt to bring men to the goodness and attractiveness which is Christ Himself. He must strive to do this through his own goodness and attractiveness.

The Christian must realize that he is dealing with man in the wholeness of his being. He must be aware that man is not only an intellectual being to be approached solely on a rational, intellectual level. Man is also physical and social with innumerable tendencies and desires which operate on these levels. These tendencies and desires play definite and important roles in his life as a human being. Through them he is drawn toward, or repelled from, things and ideas and persons, sometimes solely on an instinctual level, sometimes in the totality of his person. The Gospel, then, must be brought to man in as total a manner as possible. The Christian cannot rely only on the fact that he speaks of the Gospel to others, formally teaches the Gospel to others, and prays for them. To draw men to Christ and His Gospel, the Christian must not only do all these things, but he must act through the total beauty and attractiveness of his entire being with its own unique personality, attitudes, and characteristics.

In our own day the voice of Pope John XXIII has been heard to speak of man as the "eighth sacrament", the sign as well as the realization of the presence of Christ in the world. As Christ lived and moved among the Jewish people of His own day, He conveyed His message of love and goodness not only by His formal teaching, but also through His attitudes, His temperament, His personality, His kindness, His demeanor. He conveyed His message and drew people to Himself through His obvious enjoyment of being with them—sharing a meal with them, gathering the children around Him, or going off in a boat with His apostles. He truly taught His Father's message through His total humaneness and humanness. The Christian as the "eighth sacrament", as the palpable Christ of today, must accomplish his own role and mission in a similar fashion. The Christian conveys the Gospel to others not only through what he says, teaches, and believes, but also and very importantly in what he *is*—through his total goodness and attractiveness. One is reminded of the statement of Emerson, "Don't speak to me, because what you are shouts so loudly I can't hear what you're saying to the contrary."

The human attractiveness of each Christian, which, despite its limitations, is an unique reflection of the attractiveness of Christ, must be realized to be an important facet of the Christian's life in society. This attractiveness can be seen as a means of loving others, of taking the effort to make oneself pleasing to others as human beings whose dignity is worthy of such effort. Consequently, through being drawn to the good, the beautiful, and the attractive in the Christian, they may be drawn to the source of all goodness and attractiveness, Christ Himself.

If the Christian of today makes a sincere effort not to disfigure the reality of Christ by his own failings, but to make himself in *every* aspect of his person an attractive witness of truth and goodness and loving concern for his fellow man, this certainly will add a tremendous impact to the spread of the Gospel. Where true love and goodness and attractiveness are discovered, something of Christ is discovered and experienced.

Discretion

A sense of Christian discretion should govern my decisions and the action consequent to these decisions. Discretion is necessary if these decisions and actions are to be in accord with my Christian destiny here and hereafter. Traditionally the reality we are discussing has been termed the virtue of Christian prudence, but since this word is perhaps not too acceptable to the modern mind because of certain erroneous connotations, we will use the word discretion. One of these connotations we speak of is the erroneous impression that prudence always means doing the cautious thing. As a matter of fact, the virtue of prudence—or discretion—will lead me to do the very bold and daring if responsible search has led to the conclusion that this is God's will.

Discretion is particularly necessary in the contemporary Church. We have stated before that there is presently a diversity or pluralism of thought and life style which was not present in the pre-Vatican II Church. The contemporary Christian has to employ a holy discretion. How does the Spirit wish him to think and act on this or that issue? Amid the diversified thought on this issue, which seems to be correct? Or if there seem to be several correct possibilities, which does the Spirit wish this particular Christian to choose for his own? These questions connected with Christian prudence are closely connected with some of the ideas to be discussed in Chapter Twelve where we will treat of life in the Spirit. Consequently, we will defer further treatment of Christian discretion until then.

7

The Christian's Personal Uniqueness

Some two thousand years ago Christ walked this earth. He preached the Father's message. He extended His mercy, His kindness, and His love. He healed the sick, comforted the poor and the needy. He forgave sins. He gathered around Him the men who would form the foundation of His Church. In these and other ways Christ was accomplishing His mission. He was redeeming the world.

Today Jesus still walks this earth. He still preaches the Father's message. He still manifests His love and kindness. He still shows His concern for the sick and the poor. He instructs the ignorant, and He administers the sacraments. However, Christ walks the earth today continuing the work of His redemption in a manner which differs from that of two thousand years ago. Then Christ was present to mankind in His redemptive work according to His physical body. Now His redemptive mission on earth is visibly manifested, not through His physical body, but through His mystical body, that body which is His Church.

The Church is the earthly, visible continuation of Jesus in His redemptive Incarnation. United with the glorified Christ the members of the Church assist Him in continuing His mission of being King, Prophet and Priest for the salvation of the world. The closeness of the People of God with Christ is brought out by the words of St. John: "I am the vine, you are the branches. Whoever remains in me, with me in him, bears fruit in plenty; for cut off from me you can do nothing. Anyone who does not remain in me is like a branch that has been thrown away—he withers; these branches are collected and thrown into the fire, and they are burnt. If you remain in me and my words remain in you, you may ask what you will and you shall get it." (Jn 15:5-7).

As the People of God assist Jesus in the continuation of the redemptive Incarnation, they continue the great sacramental sign which Jesus Himself was in His historical existence. Through His human enfleshment Christ was the visible or sacramental manifestation that God had thrust Himself so intimately into man's world. The historical Christ was the sign of God's mercy and love towards us. He was the sacrament of God's loving presence among us. He was the sacramental sign that God had irrevocably given Himself to men.

The Church, since she is in space and time the continuation of the Incarnation, is also the sacrament, the visible manifestation, of God's salvific presence in the world. After Christ, Who is the primordial sacrament, the Church is the great sacrament of God. She is the terrestrial sign that the redemptive Incarnation is a continual process, one which will endure until the end of time. One function of the Church as sacramental witness of God's salvific purpose in Christ is to remind the *People of God themselves* that there is this mighty and urgent task to be accomplished—to assist Christ in bringing His redemptive mission to completion.

As members of the Church, we assist Christ with His salvific process in different ways. St. Paul tells us: "Just as a human body, though it is made up of many parts, is a single unit because all these parts, though many, make one body, so it is with Christ." (I Co 12:12).

". . . God put all the separate parts into the body on purpose. If all the parts were the same, how could it be a body? As it is, the parts are many but the body is one. The eye cannot say to the hand, 'I do not need you', nor can the head say to the feet, 'I do not need you'." (I Co 12:18-21).

"Now you together are Christ's body; but each of you is a different part of it. In the Church, God has given the first place to apostles, the second to prophets, the third to teachers; after them, miracles, and after them the gift of healing; helpers, good leaders, those with many languages. Are all of them apostles, or all of them prophets, or all of them teachers? Do they all have the gift of miracles, or all have the gift of healing?" (I Co 12:27-29).

These words of Paul remind us that there are multiple tasks to be performed in the life of the Church. Some are to be teachers, some leaders, some follow one vocation, some follow another. Yet there is a further truth to be aware of. There are multiple differences even in the way the same task or vocation is exercised in the Church. For example, among those who are teachers, each will be a teacher according to his own personal gifts, temperament, and uniqueness. This fact leads us to the inevitable conclusion that each Christian has an unique role or mission to fulfill. This uniqueness of one's mission is simply a logical consequence of the fundamental uniqueness of each individual.

Each person is an unique expression of God's crea-

tive love. Each person can truthfully say to himself that
there has never before been anyone like himself, there
is no one like him now, and there never will be in the
future. As God gives each person this radical uniqueness, He attaches to it an unique mission or role to be
accomplished. Cardinal Newman tells us: ". . . everyone
who breathes, high and low, educated and ignorant,
young and old, man and woman, has a mission, has a
work. We are not sent into this world for nothing; we
are not born at random . . . God sees every one of us;
He creates every soul, He lodges it in the body, one by
one, for a purpose. He needs, He designs to need, every
one of us. He has an end for each of us; we are all equal
in His sight, and we are placed in our different ranks
and stations, not to get what we can out of them for
ourselves, but to labor in them for Him. As Christ has
His work, we too have ours; as He rejoiced to do His
work, we must rejoice in ours also."[1]

Because of the uniqueness of each Christian's existence and mission, he presents Christ with an unique
opportunity. Each Christian has the vocation to offer
Christ his humanity so that Jesus can reincarnate Himself in a new way. Christ wants to continue His redemptive work through the not-to-be-repeated newness
which is each Christian's uniqueness. To the extent that
the Christian offers his humanity to Jesus, to this extent
He has an unique opportunity to continue the redemption, an opportunity which no one else can offer Him.
To the extent the Christian fails to offer his humanity
to Christ, to this extent Jesus loses *this* opportunity
which is *this* Christian's uniqueness.

Each of us, consequently, no matter what his state

[1] John Cardinal Newman, *Discourses Addressed to Mixed Congregations* (London: Longmans, Green and Co., 1906), pp. 111–112.

of life and work may be, has the great privilege and the great responsibility to utilize his life properly according to God's Christic design. No one else can fulfill your mission or my mission, just as we in turn cannot accomplish that of another. At times we can become somewhat fearful over the life task God has entrusted to us, and as we more deeply realize the greatness God calls us to, we become hesitant as to whether we can properly fulfill our role and achieve our God-appointed greatness in Christ. Perhaps at such times we feel as did Jeremiah the prophet when Yahweh called him: "The word of Yahweh was addressed to me, saying, 'Before I formed you in the womb I knew you; before you came to birth I consecrated you; I have appointed you as prophet to the nations.' I said, 'Ah, Lord Yahweh; look, I do not know how to speak: I am a child!' But Yahweh replied, 'Do not say, "I am a child", Go now to those to whom I send you and say whatever I command you. Do not be afraid of them, for I am with you to protect you—it is Yahweh who speaks!' " (Jer 1:4-8).

Jeremiah initially shrank back from the mission God was giving him. He complained that he was not capable of accomplishing it. God answered him and told Jeremiah he was perfectly capable of fulfilling his appointed role, for He, God, would be with Jeremiah. God would work through Jeremiah, and Jeremiah's part was to be open to God, not to thwart His action, but to allow Yahweh to work through him according to His will.

All of us no doubt have at times reacted to God's call as did Jeremiah originally. Perhaps it was at the time when God was calling us to our basic state of life. Once within our fundamental vocation, we have from time to time fearfully been tempted to resist God's call to higher things, to a more complete accomplishment of our life's mission, and to a greater Christian maturity. If we ultimately acted as did Jeremiah and controlled our fears and gave ourselves trustingly to God's will for us, then we became existentially convinced that God never requests anything of us without giving us abundant grace to accomplish His design, that to answer God's call as consistently as possible is the only true path to peace, happiness and fulfillment despite the pain involved.

We are aided in remaining faithful to the unique mission or role in life which God has given us if we try to remain aware of the great value of *one* life to Christ, to the Church, and to the world. History tells us what a difference just one life can mean to the work of the Church. We have outstanding examples from all walks of life. Surely the Church has been enriched and countless lay people have been inspired because of a man named Thomas More. Here was a layman who realized the deepest meaning of life—and he did not fail to confront the true purpose of man's existence, even when that confrontation meant the giving up of his life for what he believed. Has the one life of St. Thomas More made a difference for the Church? And there are the examples of the great men and women who established religious orders and congregations. Has not each of their lives made an overwhelming contribution toward a better Church and a better world? Did it make any difference whether a man eventually called Pope John XXIII so admirably fulfilled his mission in life? Surely the world is so much better for Pope John having given it his love and kindness and joy and constant concern. And for all we know perhaps the mother of Pope John, who lived no doubt such a hidden life, but who raised her son to be what he was, made a greater contribution in God's eyes than did her son himself. And would not the world be poorer if Dr. Thomas Dooley had not been the deeply dedicated man that he was? Here is the case of a man afire with a sense of Christian mission. And he spent himself entirely in accomplishing it. Does the manner in which one life is lived make a difference?

At this point certainly many will object that the above examples of men and women are cases of people who achieved outstandingly in the external order and whose lives commanded great public attention either in the Church or the world or both. People who point out this fact object that their lives are so very ordinary, so hidden, so incapable of making headlines. Surely this kind of life does not make much of a difference to Christ, to the Church, and to the world. Surely it does not much matter whether a person living this kind of very ordinary existence fulfills his God-given mission or not. At first, many of us would tend to agree with this type of reasoning, a reasoning which is really the opposite temptation to that which we considered when we likened ourselves to Jeremiah. In that context there was question of being tempted to do nothing because we feared the greatness to which we were called. In the present case it is a question of being tempted to do nothing because we think we really have nothing to contribute. But as we begin to reflect in mature faith, we soon see the fallacy of this objection. For we realize that it is not great external accomplishments or a life which attracts public attention which, as such, make that life great and really worthwhile. If a Christian life which is characterized by notable external achievement is really great and meaningful for mankind, we know that it is so because this external achievement has sprung forth from an attitude of deep faith and hope and love. This is our ultimate answer, then, to the above objection—every Christian's life, no matter how ordinary in its external framework, can be tremendously important and make an outstanding contribution toward continued redemption, as long as that life is one of deep faith and hope and love.

God's ways are not always our ways and His thoughts are not always our thoughts. He can take a life which seems so ordinary, so prosaic, so uneventful, and achieve wonders with it as long as the person is trying to fulfill his role in life, and is open to God's guidance in the accomplishment of that mission. We cannot, then, use the ordinariness of our lives as an excuse for not making our existence really great, really significant for Christ and man—a life which really makes a difference. Karl Rahner has words for us when the ordinariness of our lives tempts us to think that our existence is so unimportant and almost useless: "Let us take a good look at Jesus Who had the courage to lead an apparently useless life for thirty years. We should ask Him for the grace to give us to understand what His hidden life means for our religious existence."[2] Notice that Rahner uses the phrase "apparently useless life". For, of course, in reality Christ's very ordinary existence at Nazareth was not actually useless. On the contrary, Jesus' hidden life was tremendously important. It was part of His redemptive effort. The apparently useless life of Jesus for those thirty years was actually an extraordinary life because of the attitude with which Jesus permeated those many hidden years. No, it is not the ordinary setting of our lives which is an obsta-

[2] Karl Rahner, *Spiritual Exercises* (New York: Herder & Herder, 1965) p. 160.

cle to our making an unique and important contribution
to mankind's assimilation to Christ. The real obstacle,
if we allow it, is our failure to relate to the ordinariness
as God intends.

There is another potential obstacle which often con-
fronts us. As we live out our own uniqueness and strive
to fulfill the unique mission entrusted to us by God,
we are tempted to want to be someone else and to have
someone else's vocation and mission. We look at the
physical, intellectual and supernatural gifts of another,
the pleasing personality of another—and so forth and
so on—and we tell ourselves that if we were only endowed with such qualities, well, yes, *then* we would
really accomplish something for Christ. In other words,
we so often fail to accept ourselves as God made us. We
fail to accept our own God-given uniqueness. We
waste so much time looking at what we do not have,
rather than looking at that with which God has endowed us. Let us once and for all accept ourselves in
the fundamental uniqueness which each of us is. Let us
develop the gifts and strengths and capacities of this
uniqueness, and let us strive to control its weaknesses
as best as possible. Let us realize that if we accept our
uniqueness as coming forth from God's creative love
and constantly strive to allow that same love to bring
our uniqueness to fulfillment, then and then only will
we achieve the peace and happiness we all desire. Then
and then only will we properly make our own contribution to continued redemption.

We have been discussing the Church's task of assisting Christ in the work of completing the redemptive
process. We have stressed that each Christian, because
of his personal uniqueness, has an unique mission to
fulfill in this redemptive effort. Each Christian is given

the opportunity to contribute as he receives his special call from God, and obviously there are varying degrees according to which a Christian may respond or not respond to God's call.

There are those who hardly respond at all, who seem to be barely Christian. They may have faith, but it is a dead faith, as they refuse to be guided by God even in serious matters. They want to be complete masters of their own existence, and the less they have to think about God the better they like it. Some of these originally may even have been given a call to magnificent Christian greatness in this or that state of life. But they turned a deaf ear to true greatness, determining to be makers of their own self-conceived greatness, and their concept of greatness never transcended the limits of space and time, as they thought and acted as if their temporal existence would extend on and on forever.

There are other Christians who respond to God essentially, but not as completely as possible. Their lives seem to be an average mixture of faithfulness to God and disloyalty to Him at times, of much good accomplished periodically, but with a considerable amount of Christian mediocrity mixed in. But they seem to be basically sincere and they do really promote the work of Christ as they essentially fulfill their roles in life.

Finally, there are those Christians who answer God's call initially and continually in an eminently generous way. They develop their uniqueness marvelously and become forceful shapers of the world's Christic destiny. Their good actions are etched very deeply within the human process, although perhaps hiddenly so. And because of them and their actions the world's goodness is more apparent, and man has approached still further towards his eternal destiny.

Today's Church needs more of this type of Christian. The Church and the world in which she is situated are experiencing a time of crisis, perhaps the most critical time of all history. But if we live in an age of special crisis with all its tremendous and numerous problems, we also live in an age of tremendous opportunity. On His part God always provides for the needs of the Church and the needs of the world which the Church is meant to serve. Surely God in this age of great need and opportunity will not fail to call Christians of all vocations to dedicate themselves completely and eminently to the task at hand. We should pray that all in their uniqueness respond as they should, making their own unique contribution to the work of Christ, but realizing that there is only one response that we can totally control—and that is our own. Each of us has to realize that especially in our present age each day is a precious gift given to us by God to help make this world more Christic. For modern man with all his problems will only pass through the present crisis successfully to the degree that he becomes more Christic, either explicitly or anonymously. For all in creation is Christic, and it exists more and more authentically in the measure that it becomes more and more Christic. St. Paul reminds us of this. Speaking of Christ, he tells us: "He is the image of the unseen God and the first-born of all creation, for in him were created all things in heaven and on earth: everything visible and everything invisible, Thrones, Dominations, Sovereignties, Powers—all things were created through him and for him. Before anything was created, he existed, and he holds all things in unity. Now the Church is his body, he is its head. As he is the Beginning, he was the first to be born from the dead, so that he should be first in every way; because God wanted all perfection to be found in him and all things to be reconciled through him and for him, everything in heaven and everything on earth, when he made peace by his death on the cross." (Col 1:15-20).

8

The Relevancy
of the Liturgy

One of the most controversial issues in the contemporary Church has been that of the renewed liturgy. A certain type of conservative says that the liturgy has been ruined, almost desecrated by the reformers. When he enters his parish church on a certain Sunday morning he may unexpectedly find himself participating in the so-called guitar Mass. None of this for him. He quickly turns on his heels. He goes in search of a more subdued liturgy, and he's willing to travel a good distance to find it. For him the guitar Mass is certainly not relevant. It does not speak to him. In fact, it only makes him angry. At the opposite extreme we have a certain type of liberal who has experienced what has been for him very intimate and meaningful liturgies. He may have participated in these on a college campus, in private homes, or in a very progressive parish other than his own. As for his own parish liturgies—well, he thinks these are the most unattractive, most irrelevant, most unimaginative ones possible. He hasn't been to any of them in months, and he never intends to be.

The two examples just cited represent the opposite

ends of a polarity. We purposely used the phrase a "certain type" of conservative and liberal. Most conservatives and liberals, while having very definite ideas about their kind of liturgy, would not react as sharply as do these "certain types". But the examples cited do point up the question of relevancy in our present-day liturgy. What is liturgically relevant for one Christian today can very easily be irrelevant for the person next to him.

To get at the problem of liturgical relevance or irrelevance, we believe it necessary to speak of the interior or invisible liturgy and the external or visible liturgy. In the remarks which follow we will limit ourselves to a discussion of the Eucharistic liturgy alone.

A few years back we heard a progressive give a lecture on the liturgy. He certainly was a person who would emphasize the need for good and meaningful external liturgy. But in the course of his lecture he made a remark which went something like this: if a person has no other choice but to attend a Mass in Latin with the priest facing the wall, he still should be able to make this a meaningful experience. Given the context, this was a rather striking statement to make. But it was based on sound theological fact. This particular lecturer, while realizing the great importance of the external liturgy, was striving to point out that the most important element of the Eucharist is in its invisible and internal dimension; and as long as there is present the bare essentials of the external liturgy, we can always have the heart of the Eucharist. Ultimately, therefore, each Eucharistic liturgy should be meaningful and fundamentally relevant to the mature Christian, even though the external liturgy may be extremely poor on given occasions. If each liturgy is to be relevant in its

inner essence, we must grasp the invisible truths behind
the external liturgy, bringing them more to the fore-
front of Christian awareness. Our consciousness of these
truths both during and outside the liturgy should become increasingly dynamic, for our growth in liturgical
participation and its influence on our lives depend in
part on such a consciousness. Let us discuss some of
these truths connected with the internal or invisible
liturgy.

The Eucharist is a sacrifice within the framework
of a meal, or, if you prefer, it is a sacrificial meal. At
the heart of any sacrifice is the concept of man offering
himself to the Supreme Being however he may conceive
that Being. This is the most essential element of sacrifice, and the history of religion brings out the continual
presence of this element in the sacrificial life of man
over the ages. This attitude of man offering himself to
God is centered in the offering of his will, and of his
entire being as directed by his will. In effect, then, when
man sacrificially offers himself to God, he is professing
his conformity in love to the divine will. He is pledging
that his existence will be guided by God, at least in
matters of serious moment.

To the extent that this attitude of offering himself
to God is absent from one's sacrificial participation, to
that extent the participation is not pleasing to God. The
history of Israel brings this out. The teaching of Israel's
prophets was in part directed at the abuse of sacrificial
formalism. The Israelites were seriously disobedient
to Yahweh's will—they were not essentially offering
themselves to Him—and yet they tried to soothe their
consciences by the multiplication of external sacrifices.
When the heart of sacrifice which is man's interior
offering of himself was lacking, the external sacrifices

of Israel were not pleasing to Yahweh. A passage from the great prophet Jeremiah brings this out: "The word that was addressed to Jeremiah by Yahweh, 'Go and stand at the gate of the Temple of Yahweh and there proclaim this message. Say, "Listen to the word of Yahweh, all you men of Judah who come in by these gates to worship Yahweh. Yahweh Sabaoth, the God of Israel, says this: Amend your behavior and your actions and I will stay with you here in this place. Put no trust in delusive words like these: This is the sanctuary of Yahweh, the sanctuary of Yahweh, the sanctuary of Yahweh! But if you do amend your behavior and your actions, if you treat each other fairly, if you do not exploit the stranger, the orphan and the widow (if you do not shed innocent blood in this place), and if you do not follow alien gods, to your own ruin, then here in this place I will stay with you, in the land that long ago I gave to your fathers forever. Yet here you are, trusting in delusive words, to no purpose! Steal, would you, murder, commit adultery, perjure yourselves, burn incense to Baal, follow alien gods that you do not know?—and then come presenting yourselves in this Temple that bears my name, saying: Now we are safe—safe to go on committing all these abominations! Do you take this Temple that bears my name for a robbers' den? I, at any rate, am not blind—it is Yahweh who speaks." (Jer 7:1-11). These are blunt words of Yahweh to His chosen people, and in their directness they unmistakably remind us what constitutes authentic religious sacrifice.

As we look at Christ's historical sacrifice we immediately see why it was perfect. He made a perfect offering of Himself to the Father. His human will was always perfectly conformed in love to His Father's will. His

life was always and completely sacrificial. Christ's entire life was included in the formal sacrifice of the Last
Supper and Calvary. Everything He did and thought
and said was included. The boyish wonder of His early
years formed part of His sacrifice. So did the days He
spent with Mary and Joseph with the many experiences
of joy and happiness, of work and relaxation, of pain
and sorrow. The short years of His public life were included in His sacrifice, with all the selflessness of that
period. During those years Christ served the Jewish
people in so many ways, and He did not count the cost.
He preached the Father's message, He healed the sick,
He comforted sinners. He gathered the little children
around Him. He wanted to do all these things and He
did them with a full and joyous heart. But there was a
price He paid. There was physical weariness. There
was the constant demand made upon His time. There
was the hatred and rejection He received from some.
There was the pettiness of others. There was the self-
righteousness of the Pharisees He had to endure. There
was the dullness of understanding on the part of His
closest disciples. As Christ experienced all this, He did
so, to reiterate, with a sacrificial attitude.

Also included in Christ's sacrifice was the way He
thrilled at His Father's creation: "Look at the birds in
the sky. They do not sow or reap or gather into barns;
yet your heavenly Father feeds them. Are you not
worth much more than they are? . . . Think of the
flowers growing in the fields; they never have to work
or spin; yet I assure you that not even Solomon in all
his regalia was robed like one of these." (Mt 6:26-29).

The friendships which Jesus had with Lazarus, Martha and Mary formed part of His sacrifice, as did His
other personal relationships. He wept over Jerusalem,

and this too was sacrificial. As one looks at the end of the mortal life of Jesus, he very obviously realizes that all the suffering and agony were very much a part of Christ's sacrifice.

Through the above enumeration of some of the events and experiences of Jesus' life, we have been striving to emphasize how the formal sacrifice of the Last Supper and Calvary touched everything in Jesus' life, how it gave visible expression to the sacrificial attitude which permeated Jesus' entire earthly life. Jesus was always offering Himself to the Father. Up to the time of His formal sacrifice—the Last Supper and Calvary—His life was a non-ritualistic sacrifice or offering. This non-ritualistic dimension of His offering was eventually caught up and included in the dynamic of His ritualistic sacrifice.

In His earthly sacrifice Christ alone was Priest and Victim. However, in the Eucharistic sacrifice, which is the sacramental renewal of Calvary, we actively participate in the priestly offering. Jesus is the chief Priest and Victim, but we are also priests and victims along with Him, as we offer ourselves to the Father in, with, and through Christ.

We participate in the Eucharistic offering to the extent that we authentically give ourselves to God, pledging that our lives are to be guided by His will. Once again, then, we observe where the heart of sacrifice lies. Our offering is one of love, for the present and continued conformity to the Father's will is impossible without love. Our Eucharistic offering is also a renewal of our love of neighbor, for so much of God's will for us is directed at loving our fellow man. We cannot offer ourselves to God in the Eucharist without re-dedicating our lives to the service of man.

Just as Jesus' earthly sacrifice included everything in His life, so does our Eucharistic sacrifice reach out and gather into it everything which is authentic in our existence. There is nothing which is really God-orientated that is excluded. As we gather around the alter, we are not engaging in a nebulous and ethereal act which has no connection with our lives, lives which are immersed so much in the here and now, lives which are made out of pain and sorrow, sweat and tears, joy and laughter, anguish of spirit, times of ecstatic happiness. Rather the Eucharistic offering is meant to gather up all the varied dimensions of life with their disparate experiences and present them ritually to the Father in Christ. As Christ's sacrifice was made up of all the happenings of a deeply human and God-directed life, so is our Eucharistic offering. The Christian father and mother bring to the altar the love and the care and the labor they have poured out upon their children. They bring the love they bear one another, too, a love which has brought moments of the deepest joy and happiness, but which also has known misunderstanding and heartache. The priest and religious put their works on the altar, works issuing forth from a celibate love, a love which experiences its own particular pain and joy. And the Christian scientist, social worker, teacher, laborer, and doctor, these along with other Christians of all works and professions bring their accomplishments to the altar. These are united to the greatest work, the greatest accomplishment of all time, the redemptive effort of Christ.

We live, and consequently make our sacrificial offering, according to the pattern of Jesus' life. Why is this? As Jesus lived upon earth, He was infusing a certain pattern or structure into His life of grace. This structure contains the various mysteries or events of His earthly sojourn. Central to this structure is His paschal mystery, His death and resurrection. Our life of grace comes to us through the humanity of Jesus. Consequently, it has impressed upon it the pattern established by Jesus' humanity when He lived upon earth. The Christian life can authentically develop only according to this innate pattern or structure. This is the reason why the Eucharistic offering of ourselves is our lives lived according to Jesus' example.

Not only do we offer ourselves in the Eucharistic liturgy according to the pattern of Jesus' life. We also draw from that same pattern during the Eucharistic celebration. For the Eucharistic Christ is present with all the mysteries or salvific events of His historically redemptive and sacrificial life. These mysteries, especially the all-inclusive mysteries of death and resurrection, are contained in the Christ of the Eucharist along with the graces necessary for their greater assimilation into our Christian existence. As we go forth from the Eucharistic altar, we carry with us renewed strength for a deeper incorporation into Christ. We are therefore able to live out the offering we have made of ourselves in the Eucharistic sacrifice according to a deepened Christic pattern.

The Eucharist which nourishes us is one and the same food for all. We receive the one Christ. The Eucharist, consequently, is a great sign and cause of unity, and this unity is grounded in love. The Eucharist as sign of unity reminds us that we are one People of God. Our individual lives, while maintaining their own uniqueness, are meant to blend as harmoniously as possible into the total life of the Church, so that we are Christians united in a common labor of love, not a people torn by jealousy, strife, or animosity. The Eucharist which we receive is also a sign and cause of the manner in which we are to live out the offering we make of ourselves at Mass; for Christ in His love for us gives Himself to us totally in the Eucharistic meal. It is a total sacramental giving which reminds us of the total giving which Jesus made during His earthly sacrifice. He gave of Himself despite the hardship, rejection, misunderstanding, and even hatred which at times He had to bear. He gave of Himself even though this meant the spiritual anguish and the physical agony of His passion and death. He gave until there was no more to give, and all He gave was imbued with a tremendous love. Christ was and is the tremendous lover. This is the deep beauty of Jesus' life. Jesus truly taught us what love is all about. According to this magnificent pattern, we are to go forth from the meal of sacrifice and give of ourselves in love to God and men. Of course, we will never perfectly assimilate the example of love, of gift of self, which Jesus has left us. But with His grace we can approach it more and more. If we do not choose Christ and choose Him more and more, who or what can give real meaning to existence? "Then Jesus said to the twelve, 'What about you, do you want to go away too?' Simon Peter answered, 'Lord who shall we go to? You have the message of eternal life . . .'" (Jn 6:67-68).

We have been emphasizing the importance of what may be termed the internal or invisible liturgy. We have stated that if the truths of the internal liturgy are understood and lived, there is no reason why any liturgy, despite all its possible shortcomings externally, should not be essentially relevant and meaningful for us. On the other hand, we should in no way underestimate the value of the external liturgy. It has a relevancy of its own, and a special power to make the total liturgy more meaningful and relevant.

There is the closest connection between internal and external liturgy. The external liturgy, or the liturgy of sign, is the visible manifestation or incarnation of the internal liturgy. The liturgical ritual sacramentally expresses the interior offering of themselves which Christ and the People of God make to the Father. The external ritual also is a sign of God's renewed self-communication to us which occurs in the Eucharistic sacrifice.

The fact that the external ritual visibly expresses the interior offering of ourselves satisfies the bodily dimension of our human nature. Man is not a pure spirit. He is a spirit incarnated in a body, and he desires to manifest through his corporeal dimension the attitudes of his inner spirit. He is continually doing this. A mother is meant to express her maternal love for her child externally, and if she does not sufficiently do this, the child can be harmed. Married love must be sufficiently expressed externally or it can become less than ideal. There must be words of kindness and other external manifestations of love and concern. The love of friendship also must be externally expressed in various ways or it can wither and die. These are a few examples which demonstrate the fact that man is meant to incarnate his spiritual attitudes.

The ritual of Eucharistic sacrifice as centered around the Victim also respects the social dimension of man as it allows us to come together and worship as members of the People of God. If sacrifice were purely an internal affair, there would be no external gathering around a common altar.

The external liturgy not only gives expression to

the interior attitude of offering. It is also meant to deepen it, and has a special force to do this if it is meaningfully implemented. This function of the external liturgy is again in keeping with the laws of human nature. Psychology tells us that the external order can influence man's interior. For instance, one who is depressed should exteriorly act as if he were happy. If he does the interior depression is alleviated.

Finally, the external liturgy is a prime example of continued Incarnation. Through the human enfleshment of His Son God has given Himself to us, and in Christ we are asked to make our response. The humanity of Christ is the link between ourselves and God. God has used the created, the tangible, the visible—the historical enfleshment of His Son—to form a profound union between Himself and us. The external liturgy is an extension and a continuation of the enfleshment or Incarnation of Christ. The external liturgy is a continued manifestation that God uses the tangible and the visible to communicate Himself and to exact our response.

If the external liturgy is a sign and incarnation of the internal or invisible liturgy, all concerned must constantly endeavor that as far as reasonably possible the external ritual is actually expressing the truths of the internal liturgy. One of these truths is that through baptism all the faithful are incorporated into the priesthood of Christ. This incorporation is brought to a greater perfection through confirmation. All the faithful—of course in a manner different than the ordained priest—have a real priestly power to offer the Eucharistic sacrifice. As much as possible the external liturgy should express the priesthood of the faithful and allow for their participation in various ways. The peoples' responses and singing are a common and obvious manner of participation. The use of lay lectors provides another possibility. Offertory processions are another opportunity to manifest the participation of the non-ordained members of the assembly. When members of the congregation bring the gifts to the altar at the offertory, this helps symbolize that the entire assembly is offering itself with the priest to the Father in Christ. These are a few examples of how the external liturgy functions as signs or visible manifestation of the truths of the internal liturgy.

In order to utilize the sign value of the liturgy to its fullest possibilities, Eucharistic celebrations should be planned as much as possible with a particular congregation in mind. Today's pluralistic Church means, among other things, that there are varied liturgical interests. This diversification of liturgical preference should be respected as much as is legitimately possible. The flexibility of the renewed liturgy often allows the celebrant and liturgical committees to respect the interests and background of the Eucharistic assembly. Sometimes this is not possible. In parish Masses the assembly is often composed of people of different ages and of varied liturgical interests. At such liturgies those responsible should plan so that the celebration will at least be acceptable and meaningful to the tastes of the wide majority. But even in parishes much can be done for the proper differentiation of liturgies. Through proper planning and publicity a wide variety can be offered the people, and the people can consequently be aware of what type of liturgy is being offered at this or that time of day or evening. The importance of all this should not be underestimated. We have stated that the liturgy's invisible truths and realities are the most important element. But we should by no means make light of the value of the external liturgy. To repeat, the visible sign of liturgy expresses the interior attitude of offering to God, and God's self-communication to the people. The more perfectly this is expressed for this or that particular Eucharistic assembly, the better that particular liturgy—and, all things being equal, the more relevant it will be.

9

Dimensions
of Christian Community

There are millions and millions of people the world over. They comprise what may be called the world community. The members of this cosmic community are supposed to live in a basic love for one another. They are supposed to be united in bonds of mutual support and interdependence. This is true because God created man as a social being. Man is not intended to cut an isolated path through life. He is meant to walk hand in hand with his brother. Because man is social he is meant to live in the society of man. He is meant to help others in so many different ways. He is meant also to realize that he cannot achieve his destiny unless he himself receives aid and support and love from others.

There is much that is right with the world community. There are countless manifestations everyday that man does take the social dimension of his nature seriously. There are doctors, scientists, mothers and fathers, businessmen, teachers, laborers, and people from all the other walks of life, who have a real social concern. They want to make a real contribution to society through their activity. They want this to be a

better world, a better world community, because of
what they are and what they are doing. Obviously not
everyone has these attitudes. But we often look too
much at the evil in the world and allow it to blind us
too much to the good. We have to be more aware of
the deep goodness which exists in many human hearts,
a goodness which helps maintain and promote the
community of man.

If there is much that is right with the world community, there is still much that is wrong with it. There
are still wars and threats of wars. There are still nations
which hate other nations. Within one and the same
nation there are so many forces working against the
ideal of community. Business and labor often deeply
mistrust each other. They too often seem to lack a real
human concern for each other. There is racism and vio-
lent crime which tends to destroy its own immediate
environment, and which adds to the moral sickness of
the total community. There are pornographers and
dope peddlers and all the other perverse individuals
who use the structures of community to destroy community for their own selfish gain. And within that most
basic and necessary entity of community, the family,
there is too often too much strife, too much selfishness,
too little love.

We have movements today which, in their own gro-
tesque way, tell us that there are many things wrong
with the community of man. There is, for instance, the
hippie phenomenon. Hippies have publicly opted to
withdraw from the great society. They feel it has no real
meaning for them. They feel modern man is caught up
in an inhuman pace of overly commercialized life. They
feel this structure no longer allows man to enter into
real human relationships with his fellowman. There is a

lot that is wrong with much of the hippie movement and with many hippies themselves. There is a lack of a real sense of responsibility in many instances. The hippie seems to forget that man must earn his bread by the sweat of his brow, that the human condition is not meant to tolerate able-bodied individuals who live off of the work of others. Often there are also gross excesses in hippieland. There is often an irresponsible hedonism, a blatant misuse of sex, a sick dependence on drugs. But if there are things wrong in hippie-land, let us not allow ourselves to deny the fact that the hippies have some of the truth on their side. They are correct in saying that there are many lies, hypocrisies, and contradictions in today's community of man. They are correct in saying that there is too little love and concern between man and man. They are correct in saying that many structures of contemporary society are destroying that society. In their own way they remind us that the community of man is far removed from what it should be, that many miles must yet be painfully travelled before the Promised Land is reached. Although their way of life is obviously not the proper solution to society's ills, they have helped direct attention to these problems.

The leader in helping form a better community among men should be the Christian community. God has established the Church as a leaven for the development of a graced society of men. The natural bonds of union among men have been deepened and elevated through the redemptive work of Christ. Despite the fact that the majority of men do not realize it, there is only one community of men, and it is Christic. The Church is the chief earthly channel of the grace which deepens the Christic image of the world society.

If the Church is to be a proper leaven for the forma-
tion of world community, she herself has to progress
in a sense of community. There must be a growing understanding of the truths and principles pertaining to
Christian community, and a growing desire to implement these truths on the practical level. Throughout
the course of salvation history God has always communicated Himself within the framework of community. In saying this we are not maintaining that God
does not communicate Himself to indviduals in a very
intimate and personal manner, respecting their uniqueness, their individuality. We are merely saying that
God communicates Himself to man according to man's
totality, and one dimension of man's totality is his
social aspect. God has respected this social dimension
of man. In His self-communication to us He has called
us together in religious community, or convenant. He
does not give Himself to us as to isolated individuals.
It seems in our present age that God is calling us to
an even deeper realization of these truths.

The Christian community is a terrestrial reflection
in time and space of the ultimate and absolute community, that of the Trinity. In a special way we are
supposed to give witness to Trinitarian life. Trinitarian
life centers in the divine knowing and loving. From all
eternity the persons of the Trinity are united in the
most intimate bonds of knowledge and love. The divine
knowing and loving have also gone outside of God and
brought about creation and redemption.

Grace, which is a created participation in Trinitarian
life, calls us to a special life of knowing and loving.
Christian faith and love allow us to know and love God
in a special manner. Faith and love also give us a new
capacity to relate to our fellow Christians, and to all

men. Consequently, the Christian community's life, just as is the life of the Trinity it reflects, is rooted in the activities of knowing and loving—of Christian faith and love. Having established this basic theology, let us now consider various dimensions of Christian community.

As the life of the Trinity is person-centered, so must be the life of Christian community. For too many years we have not been sufficiently person-conscious. However, the theology emanating from Vatican II is rectifying this situation. In the pre-Vatican II Church we too often tended to make structures in the Church ends rather than means to serve the persons of the Church. Slowly but surely structures are being renewed so that they may serve their true purpose. Structures in the Church are meant to aid in the total development of the Christian person.

Community, in turn, develops as the persons comprising that community develop as authentic Christian personalities. Just as each divine person contributes perfectly to the community life of the Trinity according to the perfect fulness of His personhood, so each Christian contributes to community in proportion to the fulness and perfection of his person-development. The Christian person develops as he puts into action his graced capacities. Consequently, the call of Vatican II for a fuller exercise of the Christian life on the part of all the People of God is, among other things, creating the environment for a deeper Christian community.

Authentic interpersonal relationships also help to develop community. The Trinitarian community is one of profound relationships. As we reflect Trinitarian community in space and time we are intended to have personal relationships not only with God, but with one another. These relationships not only unite the persons directly involved in a deeper knowledge and love. If they are what they should be, these relationships also make a person more capable of loving others more deeply, and therefore more capable of deepening the bonds of the total community. For a person to grow in the capacity to love his wife, or children, or friend means that he is growing in his capacity to love others also, both those who are members of the Christian community and those who are not.

Because of the limitations of time and psychic energy, because of difference in temperaments, and for various other reasons, we can have deep personal relationships with only a relatively few persons within the Christian community. But as much as possible we should also take the means and effort to know better and love more fully the other members of the community with whom we have contact in one form or the other. It is somewhat sad to observe what happens too often in too many Catholic parishes Sunday after Sunday. Many come and go to the liturgy without any apparent interest even to exchange a simple hello with the others with whom they are intimately united in Christ in offering the Eucharist. This is merely one example. Other examples concerning parish life, diocesan life, religious life, and family life could be cited which point up the lack of communication between various members of the Christian community. These examples indicate that we are still too much unaware of the obvious—that one way in which community grows is through communication based on knowing and loving the other.

Another dimension of Christian community is its function of witness. Just as Christ was the visible witness to the Father's truth, so likewise the People of

God must continue that witness. United with Jesus, we are the visible extension of the now invisible Christ. We are the Christ that the world sees and hears and touches. Among the various truths of Christ to which the Christian community witnesses, certainly a central place must be given to love. God's love above all is manifested through the enfleshment of Jesus: "Yes, God loved the world so much that he gave his only Son, so that everyone who believes in him may not be lost but may have eternal life." (Jn 3:16). The Christian community on all levels and in all its component parts must have a special desire to live Christian love and to manifest it. The universal Church, the diocese, the parish, the Christian family, the religious community, all of these must be constantly examining themselves according to the norms of Christian love. They must be asking themselves if love, the controlling force of Christianity, is being properly reflected through their Christian existence. We all know countless examples which do portray the Christian community as a community of love. There is a history, marvelous and brilliant at times, showing how Christians of all vocations have spent themselves for one another and for mankind in general. In so many ways the Christian community has exercised the corporal and spiritual works of mercy.

But in all honesty we know that there is a darker, unattractive side to our history. Far too often the Christian community has failed to witness to love properly. For example, we have lagged far behind in certain parishes and dioceses on the racial issue. We have to admit that certain Christians have apparently not yet comprehended what it means to say that Christ died for all men—black, white, red, yellow. How else explain, for instance, the sad fact that certain white Catholics in our own age have refused to receive the Eucharist from the hands of a black priest? We wonder if these people have ever reflected on the fact that heaven will be completely integrated. We also are aware that white Christian neighborhoods have blocked open housing. Each of us could add to the list of the Christian community's failure to witness properly to Christian love. We cannot undo these many failures. We can only use them as a motive to make amends for the future. Each of us has to resolve for himself that he will do his best not to contribute to any betrayal of the Christian community's responsibility to witness to the truth of Christ, especially to love.

In speaking of the witness dimension of the Church, we should briefly discuss religious life, which is a sub-community within the overall Christian community. According to the theology of Vatican II and the writings of such contemporary theologians as Karl Rahner, a witness value is one of the main contributions which the religious vocation makes to the life of the Church. Vatican II states: "The profession of the evangelical counsels, then, appears as a sign that can and ought to attract all the members of the Church to an effective and prompt fulfillment of the duties of their Christian vocation. Since the People of God have no lasting city here below, but look forward to one that is to come, the religious state, whose purpose is to free its members from earthly cares, more fully manifests to all believers the presence of heavenly goods already possessed here below . . . The religious state clearly manifests that the kingdom of God and its needs, in a very special way, are raised above all earthly considerations."[1]

[1] Vatican II, *Dogmatic Constitution on the Church*, No. 44.

To understand more thoroughly why the religious state is to give such a witness, let us look at Christ's own life. Although Christ immersed Himself so intimately into the Jewish life of His times, He did give up certain values which man considers so great. Christ did not dispose of His own life by an independent determination of how man was to be redeemed. He conformed His will to the Father's will. He lived a life of obvious simplicity. He was not a man Who possessed riches. Also, He did not marry. Through this type of life Christ pointed to the ultimate reason of His being so intimately with men. He wanted to draw them, to convert them anew, to the transcendent God. By the manner of life He chose, Jesus emphatically told man that there is something beyond marriage and riches and the free disposition of one's life, something beyond art and culture, something beyond all human values. By giving up certain earthly values, Christ was not condemning these values, for in His Incarnation He was drawing them to Himself and elevating them to a new level of existence. But through His kind of life Jesus puts before us this undeniable message: all the various values which surround us—marriage, material possessions and all the rest—are not ends in themselves, but means or aids to the living of our life of grace in this earthly and human condition. Man, to the extent that he involves himself with these various human and temporal values, must be directed by God's will. All the various incarnational values which surround man have the purpose of leading him to a closer union with the transcendent God, a union which has its very real inception here upon earth, but which reaches its culmination only in the beatific vision.

Religious continue in a special way this witness which

Jesus gave through His temporal life. Religious witness to the fact that God has become immanent in this world through Christ to give man a new life of transcendence, the life of grace. Through the human values they have chosen not to enjoy, religious are a constant reminder that there is something above all human values. They remind us that Christ in His revolutionary role, His role of conversion, has redirected anew man and his values towards the transcendent God. Religious give witness to the power of God's Christic love to seize certain Christians and inspire them to give up gladly what is so dear to man's heart—marriage, the opportunity for unlimited material possessions, and the free disposition of one's life. This special witness or manifestation of God is meant to be brought by religious to all types of temporal engagement—teaching, scientific research, nursing, social work, and the rest. In summary, let us emphasize that we are not maintaining that witness is the only function of religious life, or that the rest of the Christian community does not witness, or that other vocations in the Church do not make their own special contribution. We are merely stating that there is a special witness value connected with that type of community which is the religious life.

Another dimension of Christian community is the sense of corporateness that should permeate the consciousness of the Church's members. We must think in terms of what is good for the entire community, and, through this community, what is good for the community of man. We must be selfless, working for the good of the whole. Even when we disagree, we do so not that we may appear to have the upper hand, but because we believe that to disagree here and now is necessary so that the truth may better emerge. St. Paul speaks to us about this sense of corporateness: "If our life in Christ means anything to you, if love can persuade at all, or the Spirit that we have in common, or any tenderness and sympathy, then be united in your convictions and united in your love, with a common purpose and a common mind. That is the one thing which would make me completely happy. There must be no competition among you, no conceit; but everybody is to be self-effacing. Always consider the other person to be better than yourself, so that nobody thinks of his own interests first but everybody thinks of other people's interests instead." (Ph 2:1-4).

In our sense of corporateness, motivated by a common purpose and a common good, we should learn to rejoice in the gifts and the achievements of others. These are not isolated gifts and achievements. They redound to the good of the whole body. We all probably know of instances of jealousy and a false sense of competition which have hindered the work of Christ. To name some possibilities, these things may occur on a diocesan level, or between dioceses, or in parishes, or in religious orders. If the work of Christ is really being accomplished, and if I am making the effort to do my part, what does it really matter whether I or someone else is responsible for this or that particular accomplishment? What does it matter whether this or that group or organization receives the credit? St. Paul again has words for us: "Brothers, I myself was unable to speak to you as people of the Spirit: I treated you as sensual men, still infants in Christ. What I fed you with was milk, not solid food, for you were not ready for it; and indeed, you are still not ready for it since you are still unspiritual. Isn't that obvious from all the jealousy and wrangling that there is among you, from the way that you go on behaving like ordinary people? What could be more unspiritual than your slogans, 'I am for Paul' and 'I am for Apollos'?

"After all, what is Apollos and what is Paul? They are servants who brought the faith to you. Even the different ways in which they brought it were assigned to them by the Lord. I did the planting, Apollos did the watering, but God made things grow. Neither the planter nor the waterer matters: only God, who makes things grow. It is all one who does the planting and who does the watering, and each will duly be paid according to his share in the work. We are fellow workers with God. . . ." (I Co 3:1-9).

Our sense of corporateness should also instill in us a sense of responsibility toward personal Christian growth. Because I am a member of Christian community, my personal actions go beyond the limits of my own individual existence. My goodness in some way is felt throughout the entire body, the entire Christian community. The evil within me also has repercussions of similar proportions. These are ideas we too seldom reflect upon. There are analogies which remind us of the truth involved. For example, we know how the good and evil actions of students can correspondingly have their effect throughout an entire school. The group effort of a football or basketball team can be hindered because just one player refuses to train properly and keep himself in proper physical condition. The case is similar with our own Christian existence. It takes a spirit of faith to be consciously aware of these truths, and it takes a spirit of love and generosity to make them operative in our lives. Indeed, to grow in the spiritual life for the sake of the other members of the body of Christ is a great sign of love for them. For to grow spiritually in

Christ demands a dying, yes, a daily dying, a mystical dying to our selfishness, to all within us which is not according to Christ.

Still another dimension of Christian community is the concept of shared activity and shared responsibility in the Church. Each member of the Church is baptized into the priestly, kingly, and prophetic activity of Christ. A real shared exercise of these offices by all the members of the People of God should be implemented on every level and in every way possible.

There has already been much accomplished in this regard since Vatican II. The renewed liturgy has enabled all the faithful increasingly to exercise their share in Christ's priesthood. Vatican II states that this is to be the primary aim of the renewed liturgy: "In the restoration and promotion of the sacred liturgy, this full and active participation by all the people is the aim to be considered before all else . . ."[2]

In the exercise of the kingly or guiding office of Christ we also have observed a noted improvement. Laity and religious now are members of parish councils and assist the pastor in the formulation and the implementation of parish policy. Similar councils or senates on the diocesan level enable bishops to enlist the talents of priests, religious, and laity in the very difficult and complex task of running a modern day diocese. In religious life there has been this same attempt to draw from the opinions and abilities of all the members in the government of the religious order or congregation.

Finally, there has been an increased participation and sharing in the exercise of the Church's prophetic office. There is a growing awareness that the Spirit with His

---

[2] Vatican II, *Constitution on the Sacred Liturgy*, No. 14.

truth is active throughout the entire People of God. To teach properly the heirarchy must always be aware of this. As the situation indicates, the heirarchy should draw on the expertise and knowledge not only of theologians, but of laity, religious, and priests who have special competence regarding the issue at hand. The great mass of the faithful should also be consulted through proper and efficient means in those instances when it would be helpful to know how the Spirit seems to be working throughout the entire People of God.

The above are just a few indications of how the People of God actively participate in the kingly, priestly and prophetic role of Christ. There are obviously many other possibilities within the Church and the world. If much has been done in recent years to increase this participation in the activity and responsibility of the Church, there is still considerable room for improvement. There is still a vast amount of unused talent in the Church. Those in a position to do so must develop the structures necessary to bring this potential capacity to actuation. We certainly have reason to pause and question ourselves when we reflect upon the Church's vast numbers. Could we be accomplishing more than we actually are?

The self-transcendence of community is another very important dimension to be considered. The Christian community on each and every level must realize that there is to be an overflow outside of itself. Christian community is not meant to be and to act just for itself. On the universal level the Church, while obviously intended to be of service to her own members, must be always concerned to be of service to all mankind. The Church must be constantly concerned about man's problems, his fears, his hopes, and must be in a dialogical openness with the world of men. This is none other than the spirit of Vatican II: "Though mankind is stricken with wonder at its own discoveries and its power, it often raises anxious questions about the current trend of the world, about the place and role of man in the universe, about the meaning of its individual and collective strivings, and about the ultimate destiny of reality and of humanity. Hence, giving witness and voice to the faith of the whole People of God gathered together by Christ, this Council can provide no more eloquent proof of its solidarity with, as well as its respect and love for, the entire human family with which it is bound up, than by engaging with it in conversation about these various problems."[3]

Dioceses and parishes must also apply the principle of self-transcendence. There is still too much provincialism with us. Why are there not more examples of rich parishes assisting poor parishes? There also could be a more effective collaboration of resources and personnel as regards apostolic activity. What applies to parishes can similarly be said of dioceses. We admit that there are limits to all this. But, generally speaking, we are considerably removed from those limits. We have not sufficiently realized what it means to say that we are *one* People of God, *one* Christian community.

We make a final application of the dimension of self-transcendence to religious life. Amid the process of the contemporary renewal in religious life, two principles have often been operative in discussion, planning, and implementation. One principle says that the emphasis should be on the fact that religious should *be*, that they should be for one another, that the personal needs of the

[3] Vatican II, *Pastoral Constitution on the Church in the Modern World*, No. 3.

individual religious should be of the utmost concern. This emphasis is a reaction against the functionary concept of religious life which was so long dominant. This functionary principle assumes that religious gather together to *do* for others, to be of service for Church and world. Under this principle religious are looked upon primarily as persons to fulfill roles and accomplish tasks.

Perhaps in describing these two principles we have drawn the lines of distinction a little too sharply, but all in all we believe the description of these two points of orientation for religious life is fairly accurate. Which emphasis is correct? Actually, we believe there has to be an equal stress given to both. All the reasonable means should be used to develop community. Mutual love and concern and support should be developed among the religious. The talents and interests of individuals should be given due consideration in the assignment of apostolic work. But self-transcendence must also be operative, both on the part of individuals and the entire group of religious. They must *do* for Church and world. They must be careful not to exhaust too much time and energy looking inward at themselves. Being and doing must always be balanced.

We have been considering some of the chief dimensions of Christian community. As these are developed in love by the members of the People of God, in various ways the entire body is maturing more and more into Christ: "If we live by the truth and in love, we shall grow in all ways into Christ, who is the head by whom the whole body is fitted and joined together, every joint adding its own strength, for each separate part to work according to its function. So the body grows until it has built itself up, in love." (Ep 4:15–16).

10

The Christian's Secular Involvement

The following Scripture passage strikingly tells us how much God loves His creation: "Yes, you love all that exists, you hold nothing of what you have made in abhorrence, for had you hated anything, you would not have formed it. And how, had you not willed it, could a thing persist, how be conserved if not called forth by you? You spare all things because all things are yours, Lord, lover of life, you whose imperishable spirit is in all." (Wis 11:24–12:1).

This love which God has for His creation centers very especially in man. God loves man so much that He became one of us. God in Christ has immersed Himself profoundly and intimately into man's world. In the Incarnation He has made Himself personally present to us in a new way. The Word, in taking a human nature so closely to Himself, tells us that man and his world have been united so much more intimately to God because of His own humanity. Christ through His own human enfleshment has assumed all authentic human values and given them a new value and dignity. He is the head of a new creation. His humanity is the summit of creation, and the rest of creation belongs to Him, exists because of Him.

Christ through His human enfleshment has freed man from sin and has elevated him to the order of Christic grace. Grace is essentially transcendent, a participation in God's transcendent life. Man, even in the state of non-elevated nature, would have opened himself to an always greater possession of truth and goodness, especially to God Who is ultimate transcendent truth and goodness. In man's elevation in Christ through grace, consequently, his openness to transcendency has been deepened.

God calls us to share in His love for His creation. He calls us to a participation in His creative and redemptive work. Our zeal and enthusiasm for accepting this invitation to assist in the world's evolutionary movement towards God in Christ obviously depends upon our love for Christ. If our love for Him is weak or mediocre, we will have little zeal to bear with the hardships which are inevitable if one is to help in the process of more deeply imprinting the name of Jesus upon the universe. The stronger the bond of love between Jesus and the Christian and the more the Christian realizes what it means to be loved by Him, the more the Christian will contribute to the restoration of all things in Christ. The Christian must constantly open his heart to the warmth of the Spirit so that the Spirit's action may create within him an enthusiasm for Christ similar to that which He inspired in St. Paul: "For I am certain of this: neither death nor life, no angel, no prince, nothing that exists, nothing still to come, not any power, or height or depth, nor any created thing, can ever come between us and the love of God made visible in Christ Jesus our Lord." (Rm 8:38–39).

The Christian zeal for deepening the beauty of the world's Christic design also depends on the love he has for his fellowmen. It takes a constant, a vibrant, a long-suffering love for others, to contribute properly to the greater Christofinalization of man and his world. Again St. Paul gives us an example. As much as he wanted to die in order to be with Christ, he was willing to work on for his brethren because he loved them so much: "Life to me, of course, is Christ, but then death would bring me something more; but then again, if living in this body means doing work which is having good re-sults—I do not know what I should choose. I am caught in this dilemma: I want to be gone and be with Christ, which would be very much the better, but for me to stay alive in this body is a more urgent need for your sake." (Ph 1:21–24).

The Christian should have a deeper love for creation than the non-believer. All that is good and true and beautiful, all that man reaches out for in hope, all the possibilities for man's true earthly progress, all the worth-while and enthusiastic dreams of man's heart for a better world—yes, all this the Christian should yearn for more deeply than the non-believer. Why? Because the Christian knows that man and his world belong to Christ. He knows that man's pursuit of the true, the good, and the beautiful is ultimately a pursuit of Christ. He knows that any authentic step forward which man makes marks a deepening of the Christic evolutionary process whereby man and his world are united more fully to the center and crown of the universe, Christ Himself.

Because the world belongs to Christ, the Christian should feel at home in his secular involvement. There is obviously a sinful dimension to the world. There are

murders and rapes and thieveries. There are seething
hatreds, gross injustices, lies and calumnies, blatant
sexual promiscuity, selfish lust for power. There is too
much serious neglect of duty, and a hedonistic pursuit
of pleasure. But the sinful element of the world should
not blind us to its basic goodness and beauty, a goodness
and beauty put there by the blood of Christ. Christ
has basically redeemed man and his world. The fact
that this redemption will only reach its fulness at the
end of time should not prevent us from seeing the
Christic image which has already been imprinted upon
man and the temporal order.

As far as the world's sinful dimension is concerned,
we obviously do not love and embrace this. A holy sad-
ness should touch us when we reflect upon the moral
depravity which defiles the world's Christic image. But
we do not refuse secular involvement because the
world's sinfulness makes this unpleasant at times. We
often have to be different from the way much of the
world thinks and acts. But we are different in a way
that does not make us shirk our secular involvement for
Christ. Gabriel Moran put it well: "Some people are
different from their society because they hate it and
wish to escape from it. Some people are different from
their society because they love it and wish to transform
it."[1]

We are situated in our secular or temporal environment in a manner proportionate to our vocation. Although there are obvious similarities in the way the lay
person, the religious, and the priest relate to the secular
order, there are also differences. There can be differences even within the same basic state of life. A clois-

[1] Gabriel Moran, *The New Community* (New York: Herder & Herder, 1970), p. 117.

tered contemplative relates to the temporal differently than does a religious in one of the active orders or congregations.

But whatever our vocation and in whatever manner that vocation basically determines our relationship to the secular and the temporal, relate we must. The bodily dimension of our human nature has inserted us into the order of the material and the tangible, the spatial and the temporal. While we do acknowledge the basic unity of man, and do not wish to introduce a false dichotomy, we must recognize that we are spirits incarnated in a body. It is through our bodies that we make contact with the secular. In the phrase of Rahner, we are spirit in the world.[2] Both of these dimensions of our nature, the spiritual, and the bodily which inserts us into a material world, must be respected, and respected *in their union* with one another, in their complementarity. Living as spirit incarnated, or as spirit in the world, is the only way in which we achieve our own redemption. It is the only way in which we collaborate with God in His creative and redemptive effort. It is the only way in which we can deepen the Christic design of man's world.

Jesus taught us all this through the manner in which He achieved His objective redemption. He redeemed us within the framework of a human life which was inserted into the secular and the temporal. He redeemed us within the framework of the human condition. He related to the secular according to His vocation, according to His mission. As we previously stated, His mission required of Him that He separate Himself from certain human values. But, paradoxically, through

[2] Cf Karl Rahner, *Spirit in the World* (New York: Herder & Herder, 1968).

the renunciation of certain secular or temporal values, Jesus was in reality relating to the secular more deeply. This is true because He was relating to His Father's creation according to His Father's will. He had inserted Himself into the secular according to this will, and He had done this perfectly. Consequently, He was perfectly related to the secular. His secular involvement was not only an actuality, but it was deep and beautiful, and precisely what it was meant to be.

The fact that each of us, in accordance with God's creative design, is a spirit incarnated in a body, a spirit in the world, leads us to the observation that our secular involvement for Christ is to be lived out within the framework or polarity of incarnationalism-transcendence. This particular framework respects the type of creature man is—spirit incarnated in body—and offers certain general principles to guide his involvement with the secular. This complementarity of Christian incarnationalism, or immanence, and transcendence arises out of the enfleshment of the Word. The Incarnate Word tells us by what He himself is that there must be both of these dimensions in our Christian existence. Paul-Marie de la Croix, in speaking of St. John the Evangelist, observes: "Like all contemplatives and mystics, John has been profoundly attracted by those two complementary aspects of the unique Reality: God's transcendence and immanence. This transcendence and immanence, present and operative in the Word made flesh, enveloped, impregnated, and penetrated him through and through."[3]

What does the thrust of incarnationalism or immanence stress? Stressed is the fact that Christ in His re-

[3] Paul-Marie de la Croix, *The Biblical Spirituality of St. John* (New York: Alba House, 1966), p. 51.

demptive Incarnation has reached out and embraced not only man, but has also united to Himself the entire temporal order. The Christian must be incarnationally involved with man and his temporal values in order to assimilate them still more intimately to the redemptive love of Christ. Created things and values must be respected in their own relative autonomy. The thrust of Christian incarnationalism points out the correct use of creatures and human values rather than their renouncement. The attitude of incarnationalism bids us to love deeply God's creation and to be enthralled with it.

The attitude of Christian transcendence admits the legitimacy and necessity of secular involvement. But it stresses that in a Christian's very involvement, he is being called to transcend the particular, the concrete, the tangible, and go out to a greater union with the transcendent God. This is God's design for himself and for all men whom he is striving to lead closer to God through his Christian involvement with the secular. The thrust of transcendence stresses that, while it is true the life of grace has its very real beginnings here below, it reaches its culmination only in eternity. Here below the Church is a pilgrim Church—and each of us with the rest of mankind is caught up in this pilgrim march. We are pilgrims because we have no lasting home here below. The attitude of transcendence also warns that the proper precautions must be taken so that the Christian's incarnational involvement will be as God intends it to be. There must be prayer and self-discipline. There must be a certain renunciation of created values, not only so that we may learn to relate to them properly, but also to allow our life of grace to develop properly. This life of grace has a thrust to seek and find God in His creation, but also, says the attitude of transcendence, our life of grace has a thrust to seek union with God as He is in Himself. Renunciation is one means of achieving this as attested to by the words of Rahner: "For such renunciation is either senseless or it is the realized and combined expression of faith, hope and charity which reaches out towards God precisely in so far as he is in himself, and without any mediation of the world, the goal of man in the supernatural order."[4]

As the Christian is engaged in the temporal order, the balance of incarnationalism and transcendence will be determined by one's vocation, by one's particular stage of spiritual development, and by the particular graces he is presently receiving. Both these dimensions are ontologically structured into the life of grace. The more we are conscious of this fact and give expression to both incarnationalism and transcendence, the more closely we become united to Christ, the Christ Who is incarnate and transcendent.

Our secular involvement for the greater Christofinalization of man and his world is aided by the realization that what we do to change the face of the earth really matters for all eternity. The shape that our graced efforts give to creation will never be erased, only transformed and brought to perfection at the world's end. The situation is similar to our own Christian existence. The shape we give to our Christ-life as aided by God's grace remains for all eternity. If we develop our grace life, if we allow the Spirit to transform us more and more while we live upon this earth, then our final transformation in eternity will be all the greater. In other words, what we do with our own personal Christian existence during the span allotted us upon earth does

---

[4] Karl Rahner, *Theological Investigations,* Vol. III (Baltimore: Helicon, 1967), pp. 51–52.

make a difference for eternity. There is a continuity, consequently, between our Christian life upon earth and that which we will enjoy in heaven. The same principle applies to our attempts to build a secular city, a world order, according to Christ. The Christic design our labors help etch more deeply upon creation will last for all eternity. The universe man hands over to Christ at the last day, it is true, will be wonderfully transformed. But *what* is transformed is the world order which our grace-inspired efforts have helped to mold. It *does* make a difference what we do with our lives. It makes a difference for ourselves. It makes a difference for others. It makes a difference for the whole temporal order.

For the above reasons, we see that the contribution the Christian makes toward the Christic development of the secular city is important in any age. Because of the special times in which we live, the importance of the Christian's efforts is heightened. We live in an age of great and numerous and complex problems, but an age great in many kinds of achievement, an age on the threshold of even greater accomplishments.

We live in a world of many contradictions. We are witnessing a material growth taking place at a rate which past ages would have thought completely impossible. Modern man has given evidence of his control over his material environment in countless ways. Man has landed on the moon and will land on other planets, too. Modern science and technology have afforded contemporary man numerous comforts, conveniences, and opportunities for progress in the various dimensions of his existence. But despite all this material progress, despite the great scientific and technological advances, there are still millions the world over who are plagued by hunger, poverty, and disease. Modern man is achieving an even greater control over life, marvelously increasing life expectancy. But he also has developed weapons which can so quickly destroy the entire human race. Because of the advanced technological age in which he lives, contemporary man can have so many of his desires fulfilled. But in the depths of his heart there is often a restless stirring, a restless desire for something, and for Someone, a desire that he cannot always articulate, but of which he is aware. Men of today live in an age which affords wonderful opportunities for deepening the bonds of world brotherhood and world community. International systems of communication, travel, and commerce are promoting a growing sense of mutual interdependence among the nations. But there are contrary signs of division also. There are wars between nations. There are internal forces of division within the same nation—division between the rich and the poor, the young and the old, division between the races. There is a cry for personal freedom the world over as never heard before, and this is good. But often freedom is being misused, and in the abuse of this freedom on the part of some, the freedom of others is being violated. There are so many indications of the love of man for his brother. Our present times are replete with examples of persons going out of their way to render spiritual and material assistance to others. But there are also countless examples of how modern man has hardened his heart towards the needs of his brother. There are too many case histories which reflect callous unconcern of one human being towards another.

The above brief glance at modern man and his world allows us quickly to view the complexities of our contemporary society. We see bright rays of brilliant accomplishments accompanied by unmistakeable signs of serious failure. We see that there are wonderful possibilities for growth and progress, possibilities which modern man can transform into actual accomplishments. But we also see the very real and stark possibility that all of this could end in a cosmic heap of ashes—if there would occur that certain deadly combination of lust for power and domination, of hatred, of misuse of freedom, of irresponsibility, of disregard for human life and dignity.

This is the world in which we contemporary Christians live, a world that is an amazing mixture of that which is good and beautiful and brilliant, of that which is evil and ugly and dreadful. We have the privilege and responsibility of shaping the contemporary world more surely according to its Christological imprint. Jesus put this image of Himself upon the cosmic order by the way He lived His human life among us. We have to aid in directing man and his values along the path made by the footprints of Jesus of Nazareth. This is not always an easy task. There are so many forces in today's world which work against Christ, His message, and the Christic order He came to establish. But are we going to shirk the challenge? Are we going to allow all the contemporary possibilities for a further pursuit of the true, the good, and the beautiful to be choked off by the forces of evil, or diverted along paths which are not worthy of man?

As we labor with Christ in helping Him bring the work of creation and redemption to completion, we should not become discouraged by the fact that man and the temporal order seem to be less Christian than previously. We should not be disheartened at the signs that Christianity seems increasingly to be a diaspora religion. We should not become fainthearted in our efforts for Christ because official Christianity may become less of an influence in today's world. Although we see these and other signs which seem to portend difficult times for Christianity, let us not, we repeat, be discouraged. We must realize that there is an external and obvious manifestation of Christianity in the world, and there is that dimension which is hidden or anonymous. Men who are not publicly professed Christians can be coming closer to Christ without their realizing it, and without our realizing it. The entire temporal order can mature in its Christianization process in a very quiet and hidden way, so much so that even we Christians can hardly recognize what is actually happening. What we are saying can be summed up under the term anonymous Christianity. There is only one world order, that which has been established in Christ. Every man is offered salvation, but this is Christic grace, Christic salvation. The temporal order of man comes under this Christic influence also. If there is to be the desired progress of this order, it is a progress in Christ. The Christic influence, then, goes out and touches every human person, and it touches every authentic human value. It touches the whole universe. Regardless of how many men realize what is happening in Christ to themselves and to the entire world order, it definitely is happening. Therefore, our Christ-orientated efforts for man and his world do really have their effect, even though so hiddenly and mysteriously at times.

All Christians are meant to contribute to the process. All contribute by a gift of themselves, all contribute according to their vocation, all contribute according to their work or profession. The priest builds up the world order by the preaching of the Gospel, by his administration of the sacraments, and by all the other countless activities of his priestly existence. The religious help in the further Christianization of man according to the prophetic witness to Christ's truth which we previously discussed. The religious helps also through the work of nursing, teaching, social work, and the other varied apostolates, both the more traditional and the newly discovered. The religious does this, not only through an individual effort, but as a member of a community. His efforts, consequently, add to the corporate efforts of the entire group, and their efficacy is thus incorporated into the extended activity of the religious family over the ages.

The laity have a special contribution to the building up of the world order because of their intimate insertion into the order of temporal affairs. Those areas which are entirely or partially closed off to priests and religious should receive their special attention and effort. Not the least contribution that the married laity make toward the building of the secular city is the rearing of their children in Christ. Dedicated Christian parents have given to the Church and world countless Christian leaders of various vocations, professions, and occupations.

As we look at the Christian's work as such, regardless of his vocation, we see how each adds something to the Christic order of things that another cannot give. There is the artist, the musician, the engineer, the politician, the nurse, the teacher, doctor, social worker—and the list extends on and on.

The activity of Christians goes on throughout the ages. It is reflected through the prism of their own particular vocation and work and contributes accordingly to the process of more deeply imprinting the name of Jesus upon all creation. This activity of Christians continues on to the end of time when Christ will receive the universe together with the labors they have poured out upon it. Then this universe will be transformed, and the saved will receive their final transformation in the resurrection of the body. The creative and redemptive efforts of God, with our efforts added, will have reached their final stage: "After that will come the end, when he hands over the kingdom to God the Father. . . . And when everything is subjected to him, then the Son himself will be subject in his turn to the One who subjected all things to him, so that God may be all in all." (I Co 15:24-28).

II

Christian Prayer

For several years after the completion of Vatican II, there seemed to occur a waning interest in meditative prayer. The Church was opening herself up to involvement with the world to a degree perhaps never equalled in her history. The *Magna Carta* for this involvement is, of course, Vatican II's *Constitution on the Church in the Modern World*. The assimilation of this new spirit of involvement took up much of the attention and interest of committed Christians of all vocations, laity, religious, and priests. Apparently there were also other reasons for this decrease in the interest in prayer. The great demand which Church renewal in general made on time and energy, the frustration often involved during this time of adaptation, the atmosphere of a certain restlessness, all these factors—and there were others, too, no doubt—seemingly made the practice of prayer, and interest in it, more than ordinarily difficult for many.

In the past several years, however, there have appeared signs of a renewed interest in meditative prayer. A growing group of committed Christians seems to have achieved a renewed conviction that the Church's renewal process and involvement with the world will be noticeably deficient unless a sufficient number of dedicated members of the People of God are persons of prayer. There are various signs of this renewed interest in prayer. Religious orders are devoting more time and interest to the question of prayer in their process of renewal. Various orders and congregations, for instance, are establishing houses of prayer where members can come for more concentrated periods of meditation and reflection. These periods may be for a weekend, a week, or longer, depending upon the apostolic work schedule and graced inclination of the individual concerned. The pentecostal movement is another sign of our times concerning interest in prayer. Whether one fully agrees with all elements and practices of this movement, in all honesty he does have to admit that the people involved seem to be Christians sincerely interested in prayer, in some cases very deeply so.

Obviously, the renewed interest in prayer is a sign of spiritual vitality, and augurs well for the future. There can be no vital Christian life without prayer. One contemporary writer puts it this way: "There is a great need to recapture the New Testament notion of prayer and to see how it is integral to the life of the Christian. What was called the 'Death of God' was simply the surfacing of the death of faith. In turn the death of faith has its roots in many cases in the neglect of prayer. It should be no surprise if we cannot see when all of the lights are turned out in a city or in a room. Again, it should be no surprise that there is a power failure in our faith and in our love if there is no effort to draw light and strength from God through prayer."[1] The New Testament's teaching on the importance of prayer is brought out very strikingly by the example of Christ Himself.

[1] John Sheets, S. J. "The Four Moments of Prayer" in *Review for Religious,* Vol. 28, May 1969, p. 394.

The Gospels often portray Jesus as a man of prayer. For example, we have the following. St. Mark observes in speaking of Jesus: "In the morning, long before dawn, he got up and left the house, and went off to a lonely place and prayed there." (Mk 1:35). St. Matthew tells us: "Directly after this he made the disciples get into the boat and go ahead to the other side while he would send the crowds away. After sending the crowds away he went up into the hills by himself to pray." (Mt. 14:22-23). In St. Luke we read: "Now it was about this time that he went out into the hills to pray; and he spent the whole night in prayer to God. When day came he summoned his disciples and picked out twelve of them; he called them 'apostles'. . . ." (Lk 6:12-13). And as one would expect, Jesus prayed in the dreadful loneliness of His approaching death: "Then Jesus came with them to a small estate called Gethsemane; and he said to his disciples, 'Stay here while I go over there to pray'." (Mt 26:36). There is no mistaking what Jesus thinks of prayer.

If there is currently a renewed interest in prayer, there is also a certain dissatisfaction with the traditional treatment of prayer. There is a searching for new forms, new methods, new ways of talking about prayer. In the last analysis, though, the search for a contemporary prayer will have to concern itself with the heart, the essence of prayer. Traditional terminology endeavored to articulate the heart of prayer for Christians of previous ages. Contemporary treatments on prayer have to do likewise for the current age of Christians. Consequently, we ourselves will concentrate our efforts on essential elements of meditative prayer. We will do this through a discussion of three dominant "attitudes" we should bring to prayer. The three attitudes of prayer we will consider are the attitude of personal presence, the attitude of Christocentrism, and the attitude comprised of the elements of worship, thanksgiving, petition, and penitence. These three dominant attitudes obviously are not mutually exclusive of one another as the Christian prays. They are meant to blend together into a harmonious complementarity.

Christian prayer is rooted in the personal relationship which exists between the Christian and the triune God. Prayer is becoming conscious in a special way of the fact that the life of grace brings one into a deeply intimate union with the Father, the Son, and the Holy Spirit. Prayer is centered in faith and love, as is the entire Christian life. Christian faith and love are new capacities or new dispositions of the person. These allow the person to encounter God in prayer in a manner otherwise denied him. Christian hope is another extremely important disposition operative in prayer. It is the chief support of faith and love.

In faith, love, and trust we are personally present to God at prayer, and reciprocally, we are receptive of God's presence to us. This attitude of personal presence is the one which should dominate prayer. In prayer we are engaging in a dialogue with the God Who is so concerned with us: "In your prayers do not babble as the pagans do, for they think that by using many words they will make themselves heard. Do not be like them; your Father knows what you need before you ask him. So you should pray like this: 'Our Father in heaven. . . .'" (Mt 6:7-9).

The personal presence of prayer is rooted in our openness to God, in our willingness to listen to Him. Our attitude should be like Samuel's: "Yahweh then came and stood by, calling as he had done before, 'Samuel!

Samuel!' Samuel answered, 'Speak, Yahweh, your servant is listening'." (I S 3:10). St. Paul offers us a similar example. "I was on that journey and nearly at Damascus when about midday a bright light from heaven suddenly shone round me. I fell to the ground and heard a voice saying, 'Saul, Saul, why are you persecuting me?' I answered: Who are you, Lord? and he said to me, 'I am Jesus the Nazarene, and you are persecuting me'. The people with me saw the light but did not hear his voice as he spoke to me. I said: What am I to do, Lord?" (Ac 22:6-9).

Being open to God in prayer, listening to Him, saying to Him, "What am I to do, Lord?", is based on the very sound theological fact that God is the one Who takes the initiative in the Christian life. This has been the manner of His procedure throughout salvation history. This is the only way it can be because of the nature of the supernatural order. Yet we never have to fear that God will fail to take the initiative. He is granting us His grace in abundance. The danger lies with us, with the possibility that we will be deaf to His call, that we will not listen properly, that our openness to Him will be marred by our selfishness.

To be open to God in prayer means to make ourselves open to His love for us. It means a willingness to allow that love to direct our lives. It means a searching for God's will. It means a determination to be more aware of the varied manner in which His will for us is manifested. That will is channelled to us, for instance, through the needs of others, through the inspiration of His grace, through the circumstances of our lives, through the commandments, and through Scripture.

Perhaps we do not often enough reflect upon Scripture as a source of God's will for us. Yet it is one of the primary ways in which God speaks to us, indicating His will for our Christian existence. The word of Scripture is truly one of the great norms against which our lives must be measured. The word of God in Scripture judges us. It judges whether we are really open to God in prayer. "The word of God is something alive and active: it cuts like any double-edged sword but more finely: it can slip through the place where the soul is divided from the spirit, or joints from the marrow; it can judge the secret emotions and thoughts." (Heb 4:12). Vatican II puts it in this manner: "For in the sacred books, the Father who is in heaven speaks with them; and the force and power in the word of God is so great that it stands as the support and energy of the Church, the strength of faith for her sons, the food of the soul, the pure and everlasting source of spiritual life."[2] In the light of such statements of Holy Writ and of the Church, it is easy to see why Scripture should nourish our prayer in various ways.

Listening to God in prayer and dialoguing with Him is an experience which is meant to touch all the dimensions of our lives. His loving will wants to guide all aspects of our existence, bringing them to a graced fulfillment. In prayer God wants us to talk not only about our relationships with Him, but also about everything else. For our relationships to the Father, Son, and Holy Spirit, made especially conscious in prayer, radically include all else. God wants us to dialogue with Him in prayer about our human person relationships, our work, our problems, our temptations, our joys and happiness, our sorrow and pain, our successes and failures, our thrill of being alive and working for Him, the

[2]Vatican II, *Constitution on Divine Revelation*, No. 21.

difficulties we may be having with the human struggle. All these various dimensions of our earthly existence are caught up into the dynamic of prayer and become part of that prayer as long as the attitude of personal presence dominantly persists.

The dialogue with God in prayer does not have to be focusing distinctly and sharply upon these various aspects of our lives which we have just mentioned. There may be a distinct consideration of work, joy, temptation, and so forth. But it need not be this way. Often the reality of personal presence—of God to us and we to Him—will be a simplified experience. In this type of experience the personal presence attitude is the only aspect of which we are dominantly aware. All the rest (dialogue about work, problems, etc.) is there, but only implicitly or obscurely, summed up as it is in the experience of personal presence.

God in prayer, then, desires our openness. He wants us to listen. He wants us to allow Him to search out with His love those hidden and unrecognized recesses of our being where we still resist Him. He wants to engrave His image upon us ever more deeply. He wants to possess us more completely so that we may be ourselves more fully, for, in one of the paradoxes of Christianity, the more God possesses us the more we authentically become ourselves. God's possession of us in grace brings our total nature to completion. Grace perfects nature, brings it to a fulfillment otherwise not possible. Our personal uniqueness, then, is brought to fulfillment in grace. Meditative prayer, in which we make ourselves open to being more intimately possessed by God, is truly a special opportunity to fulfill our search for personal authenticity—for becoming more ourselves.

From all that we have stated it is obvious that the

personal presence dimension of prayer includes the element of our response. God is personally present to us in prayer in a fresh approach of love. He speaks to us, hoping to elicit our fresh approach of love toward Him—our response. This response is meant to take place not only during the time of prayer. Rather the response of prayer is intended to influence our total Christian existence. If we have glowing thoughts and lofty feelings about God during prayer, yet these have no real influence on our lives at other times, then our prayer is deficient. Effective prayer, on the other hand, gives a love and determination to the will and a light to the intellect which remain with us in a proper fashion throughout the day. Fully authentic meditative prayer helps shape us to be contemplatives in action.

The personal presence aspect of prayer is centered in Christ. The attitude of Christocentrism, consequently, should also permeate our prayer. The reason why our experience of God in prayer and our concomitant response is rooted in Christ is the fact that Jesus in His humanity is the Mediator of Christianity. St. John portrays the mediatorship of Christ in these words. Jesus is addressing Nicodemus: "No one has gone up to heaven except the one who came down from heaven, the Son of Man who is in heaven; and the Son of Man must be lifted up as Moses lifted up the serpent in the desert, so that everyone who believes in him may not be lost but may have eternal life." (Jn 3:13-16). God's self-communication to us and our response always takes place in and through Jesus. This truth pertains to the practice of prayer as it does to any other aspect of the Christian life.

In and through Christ God has spoken definitively to us about Himself and His salvific plan for man. It is the constant privilege and task of the Church and individual Christian to strive for a deeper understanding and a more vital assimilation of this mystery of Christ.

The theology of prayer must incorporate these basic truths of the Incarnation. In prayer we must listen to God speak to us through the events and words of Jesus' life. In this regard we see the value of often allowing our prayer to rise out of the pages of the New Testament. However, we should not mistakingly think that we always have to be sharply and vividly aware of Christ and His mysteries during prayer. In some way He always is the center of prayer, but the consciousness of His humanity at times can fade very much to the background as we are taken up with the thought of the divinity itself or some other divine truth, or with the application of God's truths to our lives.

As we explained in some detail in the very first chapter, the mysteries of Christ's historical existence are not mere past events. They very dynamically live on in the glorified humanity of Jesus. As we encounter Christ in prayer and otherwise, we are making contact with these mysteries, especially the paschal mystery of death-resurrection. In prayer, as we contemplate Christ in His mysteries, we are meant to incorporate these more vitally into our own Christian existence. We are meant to gaze upon Jesus of Nazareth and deepen the understanding of our own lives in the light of His. We are meant to reflect upon the manner in which the events of His life can be more consistently and more dynamically reflected in our own Christian existence. In prayer we are deepening the conviction that Jesus has the meaning to life. We come to realize more existentially that the parts to life's puzzle never really fit together without Him. We realize that without Him there is no really consistent unity to all the work and play, success and failure, happiness and joy, pain and sorrow. In prayer we are meant to come to a deeper realization of what Christ meant when He said: "I am the Way, the Truth, and the Life." (Jn 14:6).

The third and final attitude of prayer we will discuss is that which includes the acts of worship, thanksgiving, petition, and penitence.

In the act of worship we recognize God as He truly is, the Creator on Whom everyone and everything depends. We realize what it means to have come forth from the creative love of God. We recognize what is due the Creator on the part of His rational creatures. We tell God that it is only right that He is the one Who ultimately directs our lives, and that He is deserving of our loving submission. St. Ignatius Loyola says: "Take, O Lord, all my liberty. Receive in their entirety my memory, intellect, and will. And since whatever else I have or hold you have given to me, so I give everything back to you to be managed according to your preference. To me give only your love and your grace, and with these I am rich enough and want nothing more."[3] As we worship God we also praise Him and rejoice with Him for what He is. We rejoice that He is infinite, all-loving, all-merciful, all-knowing, omnipotent, full of all goodness and beauty and truth. We rejoice that this God is our God, and resolve that we shall not have false gods before Him, whether those false gods be our own egotistic pride, or the misuse of money, sex, pleasure, social status, or whatever.

Our prayer should also be permeated with a spirit

[3] *Spiritual Exercises of St. Ignatius Loyola,* translated by Lewis Delmage, S. J. (New York: Joseph F. Wagner, Inc., Publishers, 1968), No. 234, p. 122.

of thanksgiving. It is amazing how we can take so many of God's gifts for granted day after day without properly thanking Him for them. A permanently blind person can remind us what a great gift sight is. Many of us can go for days and weeks and months without ever thanking God for such a marvelous gift. The same holds for all the other gifts of our human nature. Then there are the many gifts of the supernatural order. God is continually giving us graces through Christ, through Mary, and the Church, through the sacraments, through human persons, and in various other ways. Do we sufficiently thank God for these gifts? Do we thank God enough for having brought us into this world, for giving us the capacity to enjoy His wonderful creation, for giving us the opportunity and the privilege to labor for Him and man? Are we truly thankful enough? "As he entered one of the villages, ten lepers came to meet him. They stood some way off and called to him, 'Jesus! Master! Take pity on us!' When he saw them he said, 'Go and show yourselves to the priests'. Now as they were going away they were cleansed. Finding himself cured, one of them turned back praising God at the top of his voice and threw himself at the feet of Jesus and thanked him. The man was a Samaritan. This made Jesus say, 'Were not all ten made clean? The other nine, where are they?' " (Lk 17:12-17).

Petition is another important aspect of prayer. We should petition God in prayer not only for our own natural and supernatural needs, but for those of others. We should never pray as isolated individuals. There should always be an ecclesial and social dimension to our prayer. As regards ourselves, the exercise of petition in prayer is a healthy sign that we realize our helplessness without God. It is a sign that we are properly humble and aware of our own spiritual poverty without God's grace. The earnest prayer of petition is also a sign of our sincerity relative to spiritual growth. If we are persistently beseeching God for this or that grace, we can be assured that we are really interested in growth in that particular area. In summary we can say that the prayer of petition is extremely befitting our status as creatures of God. We can remind ourselves what a gracious invitation to its practice Christ has extended: "Ask, and it will be given to you; search, and you will find; knock, and the door will be opened to you. For the one who asks always receives; the one who searches always finds; the one who knocks will always have the door opened to him." (Mt 7:7-8).

Penitence, or the realization of having sinned, coupled with a sense of sorrow, should also make itself felt in our prayer. This should not occur in a gloomy way or in a process of self-depreciation. It should take place in a spirit of humility. We have stated previously that humility is truth. It allows us to recognize our gifts as coming from God, and it also bids us to admit to our sinfulness. If we do not do this, we are untruthful, for none of us is without sin. If we do not honestly face our sinfulness in prayer, we will not make the proper resolutions and petitions for grace relevant to this sinfulness. We do all this in a spirit of peace, without anxiety, confident that God will not allow our sinfulness to disrupt our intimacy with Him in prayer as long as we are sorry for the past and are presently taking the reasonable means to control our sinful tendencies. We should also want to share in the spirit of the saints. They built upon their sinfulness. To help make up for their sins they pledged God a greater love, and a more selfless service toward mankind.

We should make a few remarks about conditions which contribute toward facility in prayer. The general, overall condition conducive to prayer is a reasonably healthy and vital spiritual life, or, in other words, the stage of spiritual development which God intends for the individual person in the here and now. The spiritual or Christian life is an organic whole. Its various dimensions mutually influence one another and the organic totality.

Consequently, our life of prayer is aided by a healthy liturgical life, especially by our participation in the Eucharistic liturgy. There also must be a reasonable Christian self-discipline which regulates the various spiritual and sense faculties. Without such a graced control, prayer can be extremely difficult and unattractive. The exercise of the Christian virtues, especially faith and love, must also be kept dynamic. A certain amount of religious reading—and Scripture should hold the first place—is also very helpful. This type of reading helps nourish the life of prayer. There should also be a certain amount of silence in the Christian's life if he is to be a person of prayer. Modern man seems to be afraid of silence. He seems to be uncomfortable unless he is surrounded by some kind of noise. This attitude keeps him from being fully human, for in any authentic human life there has to be a certain amount of time given to meditative reflection so that one will come to know what it means to be a man. The nature of the Christian life deepens this need for reflective silence. As Rahner puts it: ". . . man has got to have a time for leisure, for silence, for turning back on himself, and that nothing else will do instead."[4] Spiritual direction

[4] Karl Rahner, *Christian in the Market Place* (New York: Sheed and Ward, 1966), p. 92.

also is conducive to growth in prayer. A skilled director can help educate in the ways of prayer and can give reassurance that the Christian is presently praying in accordance with his present stage of spiritual growth. Lastly we mention as a condition for good prayer some kind of plan of life. Many dedicated Christians want to pray and could make real progress in prayer. Yet they fail to do so because there is lacking in their lives a minimal structure of daily life which would allow them to schedule times of prayer.

There is the final question of methods and forms of prayer. The very important fact we should always remember about these is that they are means to an end. They are means to enable us to get at the heart, the essence of prayer. In this chapter we have attempted to treat of the heart of prayer in terms of three dominant attitudes. Some today seem dissatisfied with the traditional forms and methods and are searching for new ones. One such form which appears to be growing in popularity is that of sharing meditation in a group. This can be a beneficial experience when it complements a more personal type of meditation. Whether we use the traditional methods, or the ones which are being currently devised, or those which are uniquely our own, we will always find ourselves gravitating toward some type of method or form or structure, however minimal this may be.

Whether we speak of traditional or current methods and forms of prayer, we must realize that growth in prayer does not always mean progression to a more advanced form or method. An example of what we are speaking about is the traditional description of growth in prayer in terms of an advancement from discursive to affective to simplified prayer. Often real growth in prayer is parallel with the progression of method or form. But it need not always be so. At times a person could remain with a lower form of prayer, let us say that of discursive meditation, and yet be progressing marvelously.[5] This is because real growth in prayer is measured by one's growth in faith, hope, and love. This growth can take place at times within a very elementary form or framework.

In conclusion, let us remind ourselves that as we grow in the practice of formal prayer, we will be growing in the capacity to allow that formal prayer to overflow into everything we do. We will be maturing in the Christian life. We will be advancing in the very important art of being contemplatives in action. More and more our entire lives will become a prayer: "Whatever you eat, whatever you drink, whatever you do at all, do it for the glory of God." (I Co 10:31).

---

[5] Cf. Robert J. Ochs, S. J., "Wit and Fantasy in Prayer" in *Review for Religious*, Vol. 29, July, 1970, pp. 521–526. Among the points made in this article, there is an interesting commentary given concerning the history of discursive meditation.

12

Reflections on
Life in the Spirit

In the fourth Eucharistic prayer or canon of the Mass we read: "Father, you so loved the world that in the fullness of time you sent your only Son to be our Savior. . . . In fulfillment of your will he gave himself up to death; but by rising from the dead, he destroyed death and restored life. And that we might live no longer for ourselves but for him, he sent the Holy Spirit from you, Father, as his first gift to those who believe, to complete his work on earth and bring us the fullness of grace." These words remind us that the Holy Spirit is with us to bring to fulfillment the Christic process begun by Jesus. The Holy Spirit is laboring in a work of love to bring the Church and the world to their distinct goal in Christ. The image of Christ, etched so indelibly upon the universe through the magnificent life of Jesus, is being deepened by the Spirit. He deepens this image by inspiring human hearts to a life of truth and beauty and goodness, to a life given over to a love of God and man, to a life which refuses to waste itself in a shallow self-centeredness. As members of the People of God we have a special obligation to be open to the design of the Spirit. While by no means pretending to be exhaustive, let us consider some of the conditions, truths, and practices pertinent to an authentic life in the Spirit.

If I am to be properly guided by the Spirit in the growth to Christian maturity, I must be aware of certain norms. I must constantly be relating my present Christian existence to these. Against the background of these norms I must be testing my actions, my attitudes, my basic spiritual orientation, to see if these possess Spirit-inspired authenticity.

The primary norm according to which I must be constantly evaluating my Christian existence is that of Christ Himself. The Spirit wants to form me more and more in the image of Christ. This is the goal of Christian existence as graphically described by St. Paul: '. . . and I live now not with my own life but with the life of Christ who lives in me." (Ga 2:20).

To be formed maturely in Christ under the gentle but sure touch of the Spirit means that we must possess an openness to the total Gospel message. We cannot pick and choose according to personal whim. We must be striving to live according to all the mysteries of Christ. An obvious example of this is the necessity of balancing properly the two central mysteries of Christ, those of death and resurrection. There has not always been this balance in the history of Christian spirituality. For many years the cross dimension of the Christian life, or dying with Christ, seemed to be presented almost as an end in itself. The fact that we should be Christians of the resurrection in the here and now, not only in eternity, was too much passed over. The fact that living resurrection in the here and now means an increased capacity for joy, peace, happiness, enjoyment of God's creation, a personal self-fulfillment—all this was too seldom mentioned. In past ages, then, the treatment of our incorporation into Christ's passion and death as a *means* to a life of resurrection *here* and in eternity was often poorly handled.

Today we have to guard against the opposite danger. Resurrection theology, so long neglected, has been emphasized so much in contemporary times that there is the very real danger that we will allow the suffering and death aspect of Christ's paschal mystery to fall too much to the background. There are apparently some people in today's Church who are claiming to be led by the Spirit and yet there seems to be no place in their thinking concerning the cross of Christ. The scandal of the cross has truly become a scandal for them: "For Christ did not send me to baptise, but to preach the Good News, and not to preach that in the terms of philosophy in which the crucifixion of Christ cannot be expressed . . . And so, while the Jews demand miracles and the Greeks look for wisdom, here are we preaching a crucified Christ; to the Jews an obstacle that they cannot get over, to the pagans madness, but to those who have been called, whether they are Jews or Greeks, a Christ who is the power and the wisdom of God." (I Co 1:17-24). Paul also preached a resurrected and glorified Christ, but the fact that he preached a crucified Christ cannot be denied.

We who live in an age of Christianity in which an affirmation of authentic human values is being stressed—and rightfully so—must be careful that this does not lead us to relegate the cross aspect of Christ to a merely peripheral position in our thinking and acting. There is no opposition between a resurrection-inspired affirmation of temporal values with a correlative involvement with the secular, and deep love of the crucified

Christ which is accompanied by an efficacious desire to incorporate the death mystery into one's Christian existence. In fact, the person who is vitally aware of the necessity of balancing death-resurrection in his life, as well as more deeply assimilating Christ's other mysteries also, is a person who is dynamically open to the Spirit. One of the Spirit's first and most fundamental inspirations is toward an openness to the total Gospel message, to the total mystery of Christ. The total mystery of Christ is so highly unified that we cannot adequately consider one mystery without at least implicitly including all the others.

If the Christian must measure all dimensions of his Spirit-guided life against the norm Who is Christ, he must also be aware of another very important norm. That norm is the ecclesial or Church framework of his Christian existence. The Spirit works within the individual Christian, but He does this in a manner which will not only bring the individual to a full maturity in Christ, but will also contribute towards the building of the entire body which is the Church. The Spirit does not work against Himself. To take an obvious example, it is not an inspiration of the Spirit for a Christian to leave the institutional Church because of its imperfections in order to serve Christ better. The Spirit in such a case would rather inspire the Christian to work for an improvement of the situation within the institutional Church. In our thinking and acting, therefore, we should realize that the Spirit always leads within a Church or community framework. We should always strive to be aware of the repercussions of our thinking and acting in reference to the universal Church, the diocese, the parish, and any other particular grouping to which we may belong. The Spirit inspires us to think and act ecclesially, and if this community dimension has but little influence upon us, this is a sure sign we are not properly open to the Spirit.

A third very important norm according to which we must measure our Spirit-guided life is that of our particular vocation and role in life. A decision or action which does not blend integrally and harmoniously with one's vocation is not Spirit-inspired, regardless of its objective worth. For a busy wife and mother to try to spend a great amount of time each day in formal prayer would be counter to her vocation, while such an action would be according to the designs of the Spirit for a Trappist monk. A Christian college student who engages in activities which subtract too much time from study is not allowing himself to be guided by the Spirit. The Spirit would rather inspire him first to a reasonable mastery of his academic life so that in the future he may be better able to serve God and man. Similarly, a priest scholar in the Church has to sacrifice many attractive pastoral activities, excellent in themselves, if he is to be true to the Spirit's guidance. The above are rather clearcut examples. There are times when the situation is considerably more complex, but it is the same norm which has to be applied.

The manner in which we have lived our vocation in the past, with all its successes and failures, is also an aspect of this vocation-norm we are presently discussing. We should be applying our past experience to the present. We can often be receiving what we think at first blush is an authentic inspiration of the Spirit. But upon prayerful reflection we soon realize that in the past when the same inspiration was acted upon it proved to be a false light. It diverted us from the vocational path which the Spirit had marked out for us. It momentarily made us less effective in achieving the role in life to which God has assigned us. It slowed down the process of our growth to full Christian maturity.

There are those three norms, then, the norm Who is Christ, the norm which is the Church or Christian community, and the norm of my individual and unique vocation. The Spirit inspires me to judge, in accordance with these norms, all the dimensions of my present Christian existential situation. Sometimes this is easy to do, sometimes this is very difficult. Whatever the case may be I am better able to achieve this if I am a Christian who prays. This fact leads us to another important condition for proper life in the Spirit.

Prayer is extremely important if one is to live maturely according to the Spirit's guidance. In prayer the Christian asks the Spirit for the light necessary to make decisions according to His will as opposed to those made under the influence of false lights of one kind or the other. The light of prayer helps the Christian to see the necessary means which should be employed for proper decision-making. The light one prays for should also be cast upon all the evidence necessary for making prudent decisions in the Spirit. In prayer the Christian asks for the grace to see persons, things, and circumstances in their proper Christic perspective. Unless the Christian possesses this kind of light, he is not able to reflect as he should on the evidence which is relevant to his decision-making.

The light of prayer should also be cast upon one's self. The Christian must examine his general spiritual orientation and ask himself if it presently is what it basically should be. In the light of prayer he must examine the motives he has for making this particular decision, or taking this course of action. Are his motives correct

ones? Or are they possibly selfish ones? Is this decision
being influenced by some sort of bias or prejudice?
Is this decision being made merely because it is the more
popular one, or because it is really the right one?

Prayer is necessary for full life in the Spirit not only
because it is a special source of light for the intellect.
Prayer is also a special source of strength for the will.
Prayer gives us the strength and courage to make what
seem to be the right decisions, even though those decisions are very difficult and unpopular ones, decisions
which may make life very hard or unpleasant now and
for months to come. Initially to make this kind of decision takes strength and courage. To continue to live by
these decisions takes more of the same. Can anyone say
he does not need the strength of prayer for all this?

As regards group decision-making in the Christian
community, prayer plays a similar role. Those who en-
gage in group discussion—and there are many instances
of this today—are doing the group a disservice if they are
not persons who are praying. Group discussion in the
Christian community is a seeking to discern what the
Spirit is asking of this group, what He intends for their
present Christian existence, what direction He seems to
be pointing in regard to apostolic activity. If not enough
in the group are aware that this kind of discussion is a
seeking and a decision-making process in terms of
discernment in the Spirit, and if not enough are aware
of the role of prayer in all this, then the entire dialogue
can degenerate into something approaching a business
board meeting.

Prayer, whether in relationship to an individual or a
group, takes on an added importance today. We live in a
complex society. We live in a world which moves at an
extremely fast pace of change and advancement. We

live in a Church which is affected by the kind of complex world in which she is situated. We live in a Church which is much more diversified in thought and life-style than the Church of pre-Vatican II times. We live in a Church which is beginning to look more to the freedom, initiative, and sense of responsibility of her individual Christians. All this means that light must be sought in prayer more insistently than ever. The Christian sense of discretion and discernment must be developed and brought to a greater maturity. Prayer is not the only means to achieve all this. But it is one of the means, and an indispensable one.

Another very important condition for proper openness to the Spirit is that of spiritual freedom. A basic freedom of spirit is necessary if we are to follow the guidance of the Holy Spirit and not succumb to a decision or path of action based on an inordinate relationship to places, work preferences, persons, one's own way of thinking, and the like. If a person does not possess this freedom of spirit to a sufficient degree, we can easily understand what can happen. A person can lack it to such a degree that he consistently blocks out the voice of the Spirit. Practically all his attention and energy is taken up with the object of his inordinate or Spirit-less desires. Or a person can possess freedom of spirit to a certain degree, but not sufficiently so. He may not be lacking in it to the extent that he does not hear the Spirit's voice. But he may not be spiritually free enough to choose in the manner indicated by the Spirit.

There are certain special applications of freedom of spirit for life in today's Church. Some need to develop a spiritual freedom which will enable them in appropriate instances to depart from past ways of thinking and doing things. Others need a spiritual freedom which will allow them not to be wedded to change for change's sake. There are some conservatives who are too rigid and therefore are not properly open to change and renewal. They seem to be unaware that Christianity is intended by God to respect the evolving, changeable aspect of man's nature. But there are also some liberals who are rigid in the opposite direction—they rigidly hold on to the concept of change and think everything must be in a more or less constant state of flux. They are not free enough in their thinking to realize that things traditional are not necessarily dead and irrelevant just because they are traditional. The type of conservative and liberal just described must realize that the Spirit desires to work in Christians who have a basic flexibility.

Another dimension of life in the Spirit tells us that in many ways the Spirit enlightens us, speaks to us, guides us, through the persons, places, events, and circumstances which are so much a part of our daily existence. This is especially true as regards persons. The Spirit can be speaking to me through the needs of others. He can also be channelling His truth to me through the ideas and manner of life of others. He certainly illuminates His truth for me in other ways, but His use of human instruments can too easily be overlooked. We must be willing to accept His truth regardless of its source. Here is another application of freedom of spirit we have just discussed. Liberals and conservatives must be free enough and mature enough to receive truth from one another. The Spirit can speak to us at times through an ultra-liberal, or through the most conservative, or through one who is not even a member of the Christian community. The Spirit is free to move and breathe and act as He will. He wants us to be alert to these various possibilities. He wants us to be able to recognize His voice, however strange may be the way He chooses to call out to us at times.

The Spirit consistently wants us to have a loving awareness of others, a sensitivity to their needs, an authentic concern for their personal dignity and uniqueness. One of the great signs of a proper life in the Spirit is the dynamic influence these and similar attitudes towards the neighbor have upon our thoughts and actions. St. John during the course of his Epistle more than once reminds us that the love we show our neighbor is one of the great signs we have to assure ourselves whether we are walking in the light of the Spirit as we should. For example, he tells us: "Anyone who claims to be in the light but hates his brother is still in the dark. But anyone who loves his brother is living in the light and need not be afraid of stumbling; unlike the man who hates his brother and is in the darkness, not knowing where he is going, because it is too dark to see." (I Jn 2:9-11).

At times in the Christian life we go off on tangents which divert us from the path of true spirituality. We can get overly engrossed in our work and forget one of the main reasons we took up that work—love for our neighbor. We can make ends rather than means out of certain practices and structures. We relate to them in an incorrect manner, and in the process we become less concerned for others, less loving toward them. At times we can even approach God in the wrong manner. We can adopt too much of an individualistic attitude towards Him, one which does not properly include an authentic concern, love, and service of others. When we go off in these false directions, we must allow the above words of St. John to call us back to the true path, the one which is Spirit-directed.

Another important truth we must be aware of for life in the Spirit is the fact that we must always strive to preserve ourselves in a fundamental peace of soul. This, of course, must be an authentic peace, not a false one which has resulted from a callous conscience, one which refuses to be upset even by a life of serious sin. We are speaking here of the peace which should reside in the hearts of Christians sincerely committed to a closer following of Christ. If we do not possess this fundamental peace of spirit, we cannot properly listen to the Spirit's voice, nor be properly open to His movements. At times these are very delicate and to be aware of them requires an atmosphere of peace.

It is too much to expect that we will always possess a complete serenity of spirit. From time to time there are periods of special stress and strain in the spiritual life. We may be encountering unusual difficulty in our work. There may be special problems involving the people with whom we live. We may be experiencing particularly strong temptations of one kind or another. Family tragedy may suddenly strike us. But even in such circumstances we have to make the effort to preserve a basic peace of spirit in the depths of our being. It is precisely at these times that we should have this basic peace in order to be open to the light, strength, and consolation the Spirit wishes to give us. In these times of special difficulty there will be what we may term surface anxiety and disturbance. This is to a certain extent inevitable. But the in-depth peace, that which is rooted in our inmost being, is always possible, and we must always strive for its preservation.

A final reflection we wish to offer relative to life in the Spirit is the conception of spiritual guidance or direction. One of the important purposes of direction in our lives is that it enables us to receive confirmation from others concerning the Spirit's action in our lives. This is an application of the communal dimension of the Christian life. In so many ways we go to the Father through Christ and in the Spirit by the help we receive from others. In the work of discerning the Spirit's action this truth has its application. We cannot always be authentically interpreting the Spirit just by our own lights.

This guidance in our lives can come in various ways. It can come through a group process of discernment. It can come through the enlightened advice of a friend. For a religious it can also be given through dialogue with superiors. Husband and wife can offer one another helpful advice based on Christian principles, advice which allows the other to follow the lead of the Spirit. However, complete and consistent help in discerning the action of the Spirit should ordinarily be sought from a qualified priest director. Besides the fact that the priest has a theological training which the non-priest usually does not have, he is in the unique position of being able to unite the offices of confessor and director.

To seek guidance is not to be weak or morbidly dependent on another. It is simply to recognize that I have a social dimension, and to open myself to receive help from others is one application of the Christian's living within covenant or community. Seeking spiritual guidance should not be construed as a process whereby another makes my decisions. One function of the director—there are others—is merely to help the person being guided to discern better the action of the Spirit so he himself can make the proper decisions. Finally, it is very important to realize that the director himself may not always be correct in his discernment, though if he is well-suited for his task, he usually will

be. This points up the necessity of using what reasonable means are available in choosing a well-qualified
director.

We have been reflecting upon certain conditions,
truths, and practices relative to our living in the Spirit.
Each of these in its own way allows us to come under
the action of the Spirit, to discern His will for us more
surely, to be more flexible relative to the unique way
He wants to form each of us in Christ as He teaches us
the ways of God: "These are the very things that God
has revealed to us through the Spirit, for the Spirit
reaches the depths of everything, even the depths of
God. After all, the depths of a man can only be known
by his own spirit, not by any other man, and in the
same way the depths of God can only be known by the
Spirit of God. Now instead of the spirit of the world,
we have received the Spirit that comes from God, to
teach us to understand the gifts that he has given us."
(I Co. 2:10-12).

13

Mother of the Christian

Present day society seems to be confused about women. In the face of our traditional "weaker sex" and "women first" ways of behaving, we find those seeking for the equal treatment of women and men. There is to be no discrimination—both are to stand on equal footing in all respects. From the direction of the fashion world we see some designing of unisex clothing, identically styled articles to be worn by both sexes. Husbands and wives are to share the duties of homemaking in a far from traditional sense. Both spend alternate hours outside the home at a salary-making job, and both alternate in keeping house and caring for the children. Both are equals in every sense and neither should be confined to what is seen as a subordinate role.

Almost in direct contrast to this trend we find another one in which great stress is placed upon external attributes of femininity. The thriving businesses of cosmetics and the fashion world leave no doubt as to what is considered important to be a beautiful woman. If a woman is well-groomed, has certain desirable dimensions, wear the "right" clothes, and is made-up properly, she succeeds in being the ideal or paragon that is sought after by current popular standards. Perhaps not in word but very definitely in behavior, the members of modern society have lost or misplaced the realization of what comprises a beautiful, feminine woman. Without this realization, all the accoutrements in the world, from the very latest Dior to the smartest hair-do and charm, will not make a beautiful woman.

This search for identity which women seem to be experiencing has far-reaching effects. Not only women themselves, but all of society is influenced by what women are. Down through the ages woman's role in society has been of central and outstanding importance.

There is a woman who can stand before modern man as the prime example of the beautiful woman. This woman is the one whose beauty pervades the totality of her being. She is the epitome of all those qualities so desirable and attractive to man and woman alike. She embodies all the greatness of love and tenderness and concern and creativity and beauty—all in abundance— which are so desparately needed in today's world. She, indeed, is the greatest of women, and her essential greatness springs from her mothering of Christ. She is Mary, the most perfect, the most beautiful, the most needed of all women for our present age.

It would be impossible to create Mary on paper, as it is impossible to so create any person. However, we always make attempts to do so, though we fall short. Our hope is that we can convey to others something of the person who is so important. And so, though in faltering language, we try to come to some awareness and knowledge of this beautiful person, Mary. Through increasing our knowledge of her as she truly is, we can come to share more profoundly in a loving relationship with this beautiful person who is our mother.

Mary was a woman who was blessed with a total

sincerity and deep sensitivity. She experienced every human emotion to the depths of her being. She was a happy woman, the happiest woman who ever lived. She shows us how to rejoice in the deepest sense. She rejoiced because God is Who He is. She rejoiced because God had chosen her, the gentle handmaid of the Lord, to be the mother of His Son. Though her life was often spent, as is ours, in the ordinary and unglamorous tasks of daily living, joy permeated all she did. She encountered all the ordinary tasks and circumstances of her life with an extraordinary love. This love took her out of herself in numerous ways. She loved God dearly and was awed at her great privilege of entering so deeply into His redemptive plan. Her heart gladdened with a deep glow that her Son would fulfill the promise of the Redeemer. Her deep and beautiful love enabled her to give herself to others in so many ways—to her friends, to her cousin Elizabeth, to Joseph, to Jesus. This gift of herself in love to God and to others was always beautifully consistent, despite the cost.

The magnificent sensitivity of Mary's person was not only manifest in her life of love and her deep capacity to enjoy all of God's creation. This same sensitivity also opened her to great depths of suffering. But though she suffered so deeply, joy and peace and happiness shone through it all and dominated her life. She is a perfect example to us of how to bear with suffering in the living out of our commitment to Christ. She was a woman who thrilled at being alive despite any of the difficulties or hardships she encountered. She showed a beautiful feminine strength throughout her life.

We have been given a lovely gift in Mary. As one of His final acts upon earth Jesus gave her to us, God's most beautiful woman, as friend, as example, and most of all—because it contains all else—as mother who dearly loves us: "Near the cross of Jesus stood his mother and his mother's sister, Mary the wife of Clopas, and Mary of Magdala. Seeing his mother and the disciple he loved standing near her, Jesus said to his mother, 'Woman, this is your son'. Then to the disciple he said, 'This is your mother.'" (Jn 19:25-26).

Some seem to feel that a relationship to Mary stands in the way of their relationship to Christ. They seem to think that Mary is unnecessary in their lives, that she detracts from the mediatorship of Christ. On the other hand, Karl Rahner says that devotion to Mary is one of the great signs of final perserverance.[1] Vatican II also assures us that Mary in no way diminishes the role of Christ as mediator, nor hinders our union with Him, but rather fosters it: "The maternal duty of Mary toward men in no way obscures or diminishes the mediation of Christ, but rather shows His power. For all the salvific influence of the Blessed Virgin on men originates, not from some inner necessity, but from divine pleasure and from the superabundance of the merits of Christ. It rests on His mediation, depends entirely on it and draws all its power from it. In no way does it impede, but rather does it foster the immediate union of the faithful with Christ."[2]

Realizing the role Mary is to play in our lives, we should be eager to deepen our personal relationship with her. We should open ourselves to her and allow her to exercise her spiritual motherhood towards us. Vatican II encourages us: "Wherefore this sacred Council, in expounding the doctrine on the Church in which

---

[1] Cf Karl Rahner, *Spiritual Exercises* (New York: Herder and Herder, 1965), p. 283.
[2] Vatican II, *Dogmatic Constitution on the Church*, No. 60.

the divine Redeemer works salvation, intends to describe with diligence both the role of the Blessed Virgin in the mystery of the incarnate Word and the mystical body, and the duties of redeemed mankind toward the mother of God, who is mother of Christ and mother of men, particularly of the faithful."[3]

Mary's spiritual motherhood has three great stages. The first stage occurred at the time of the Incarnation. As Mary conceived Christ by the power of the Holy Spirit, she conceived us in a spiritual manner. The second stage of Mary's motherhood towards us took place upon Calvary. There, as she perfectly conformed herself to God's will in the death of Jesus, amid the most anguished birthpangs she brought us forth to supernatural life. In heaven she continually exercises the third stage of her motherhood as she intercedes for all the graces necessary for our existence in Christ.

We can learn something of Mary's maternal disposition towards us by considering truths pertinent to a mother's relationship to her child in the natural order.

No matter what age one attains, he always can be beneficially influenced by his mother. A mother's gift of herself extends over a lifetime. True, the early years of childhood and adolescence require the attention of a mother in a special manner. But for an adult to say that he no longer has any kind of need for his mother, that he can no longer learn from her, that she can no longer be a healthy influence in his life—to say all this is to deny the great good numberless grown children have derived from a continuing healthy, adult relationship with their mothers. As regards Mary the same principle applies. No matter how mature we become in the

[3] *Ibid.*, No. 54.

166 SPIRITUALITY FOR MODERN MAN

Christian life we should never think that Mary is no longer necessary for us. The history of the saints tells us just the opposite. The saints to the end of their earthly existence had a deep and tender devotion to Mary. As their spirit of faith deepened over the years, so also did their realization of what a great gift of God is Mary. They became increasingly aware of the great role God has given her in the life of the Christian.

It is said that a mother is most clearly understood in terms of love. It is impossible to think of a good mother without immediately thinking of a loving mother. The love of a mother is shown in so many countless ways. It is shown in the loving acceptance of the pains of child-bearing. It is shown in the daily expenditure of the time and energy necessary for the proper care of a home and family. Maternal love manifests itself in the sleepless nights spent at the bedside of the seriously ill child. A mother's love also prompts her to sacrifice all sorts of material advantages for herself to help provide for the education of her children. This description of how a mother's love shows itself could be endlessly extended. But it is unnecessary to do so, for, again, we instinctively think of love when we think of a mother. And so it should be when we think of Mary. The love which Mary has for each of us is many, many times greater than the love of any mother the world over. This love of Mary is an operative love. She, too, has manifested her love for us in numerous ways. She has proved her love for us through deep suffering—that unspeakable anguish which was hers upon Calvary. She shows her love for us in a constant concern for all our authentic needs. She thinks of us constantly. She insistently intercedes for us before God, even though we might at times hardly think of her. Her love for us is deep, so intimate and personal, so warm and tender, so everlasting.

Mary's unfathomable love for each of us should be an inspiration for a great sense of trust in her. We should feel utterly secure in her care. Is not this the way sons and daughters instinctively relate to their earthly mothers? If we have but a faint confidence in Mary and do not look upon her as a great source of security, then our relationship with her is certainly not what God intends it to be. We are missing a great source of comfort in the spiritual life. Over the centuries of Christianity countless men and women of all vocations have approached Mary in a special way during the time of their greatest needs. They sought her out as a secure haven in time of severe temptation, in the hour of sorrow or depression, at the occurrence of family tragedy, in the grips of dreaded expectation. Whenever they sought her out, they were not disappointed. The Mary they approached is our Mary also.

A good and wise mother accepts her children as they are. She does not condone their faults and shortcomings, but she goes beyond these to the heart of her children's personhood. In her loving acceptance of the core person she hopes to bring the child to a greater maturity, to a greater control of his faults, and to a proper development of his capacities and unique talents. She realistically appraises these talents. She doesn't expect her child to become a doctor if the necessary intellectual acumen is obviously lacking. Mary, too, accepts us. She doesn't approve of our sinfulness. She doesn't approve of our wasting opportunities to become better Christians. But she does not reject the core person because of this. Rather she loves us mightily, and through this love she wants to aid us in controlling our sinfulness and in developing the Christian virtues. Also, she does not expect us to fulfill a role in the Church and world for which we lack the proper talent. She does not expect us to follow a path of sanctity destined for someone else. But she does want us to realize that each of us is called to a Christian greatness, hidden though it may be. Briefly, as does any good mother, Mary wants us to develop our potential. She wants the best for us in our total Christian development.

Good children, regardless of their age, want to share with their mothers. How they share will depend on their age and various other circumstances. But they know that a proper love relationship between a son and a mother or a daughter and a mother is one most conducive to sharing. The son or daughter really enjoys being with the mother. They feel completely at home with her. They want to do things with her and the rest of the family. What they do may be something very simple and ordinary in its outward appearances. But the fact that it is done in the company of a mother who deeply loves and is deeply loved in return can make these experiences very special. We are all sons and daughters of Mary. She is our spiritual mother. If we have established the proper relationship with her, we should love her company. We should want to share with her. She certainly wants to share with us. We should want to talk to her about our joys and accomplishments, about our failures, problems, and sufferings. We should want to discuss with her our plans, as we ask her for light and strength to implement them according to Christian truth.

All good mothers teach their sons and daughters in so many ways. Mary is no exception. Of all mothers she has the greatest and noblest educative task. Her maternal role is to form Christ in us, to teach us to put on Christ more and more. Her own life is itself a school for learning about the putting on of Christ.

One of the great truths Mary's life teaches us is that of complete dedication to Christ and to His cause. As contemporary theology has pointed out, Mary's virginity is a sign of this complete dedication to God, to Christ. Her virginity is a sign of her complete openness to God's plan for her. In the annunciation scene Mary declares this complete dedication and openness: " 'I am the handmaid of the Lord,' said Mary, 'let what you have said be done to me.' " (Lk 1: 38). Mary's virginity is obviously a sign of complete dedication to God not only for celibates in the Church, but also for non-celibates. It is a sign and inspiration for all the members of the People of God to live out their commitment to Christ. Actually, through baptism we pledge ourselves to such a dedication.

We cannot live out our dedication to Christ and His redemptive work as perfectly as Mary. Her capacity for dedication to Christ, flowing out of her fullness of grace, far surpasses our limited capacities. But through her example and intercessory role we can achieve a high degree of commitment. Too often we fall short of what our dedication to Christ should be. There are various reasons for this. Perhaps we give in to discouragement. We may allow the life of prayer to fade until it becomes practically non-existent. We may become overinvolved in external activity to such an extent that the Christic orientation of our lives becomes very feeble. Whatever these causes which militate against complete dedication may be, we have to put forth a constant effort to control them. We have to reconvince ourselves that, as Mary had her earthly task, so we have ours. Each of us has an important role, an unique one, one which God has given us in Christ, one which is worthy of our complete love and dedication.

Mary's virginity has another sign value for us.[4] The virgin birth of Jesus is a striking reminder that our salvation is a totally free gift of God to us. The fact that Mary conceived Jesus not by means of the seed of a human father, but through the overshadowing of the Holy Spirit, is a vivid sign that it is God Who has accomplished our salvation. This gets right at the heart of the supernatural. It points out how helpless we are without God's grace. It tells us that God in His mercy and love has taken the initiative in loving us. These truths, contained in the sign of Mary's virginity, keep us steeped in a proper Christian humility as we commit ourselves to the work of Christ. We are reminded that without God we are nothing, but that with Him and in Him we can do all things.

Mary's life also tells us that we will not always understand as well as we would like the way in which God's providence here and now directs our following of Christ. This is brought out by that event in Mary's life which saw her temporarily lose Jesus. We know the story well. The Holy Family had gone to Jerusalem to celebrate the Feast of the Passover. On their way home Joseph and Mary discovered that Jesus was not with them. They thought He might be among relatives and acquaintances. But their search proved fruitless. Finally they returned to Jerusalem to look for Jesus: "Three days later, they found him in the Temple, sitting among the doctors, listening to them, and asking them questions; and all those who heard him were astounded at his intelligence and his replies. They were overcome when they saw him, and his mother said to him, 'My child, why have you done this to us? See how worried

[4] Cf Joseph Ratzinger, *Introduction to Christianity* (New York: Herder and Herder, 1970), 210–211.

your father and I have been, looking for you.' 'Why were you looking for me?' he replied 'Did you not know that I must be busy with my Father's affairs?' But they did not understand what he meant." (Lk 2:46-50).

Mary did not understand the action of Jesus. She knew that somehow this was God's will, but she did not comprehend why it had happened. Despite her keen spiritual vision she was puzzled. But she did not rebel over the situation. Rather she conformed herself perfectly to God's will.

If Mary was puzzled by the way God's will had manifested itself on this occasion, why should we be surprised if at times we cannot begin to understand the manner in which God's will enters our lives? Her capacity for spiritual perception was far greater than ours. When God's will puzzles us we should react after the example of Mary. We should accept His will in love, however deep may be the suffering involved. To rebel would only cause bitterness, to rebel would make us less a person, to rebel would be to waste suffering.

The suffering which Mary experienced in the event just described was not an isolated instance. The prophecy of Simeon reminds us of this: "As the child's father and mother stood there wondering at the things that were being said about him, Simeon blessed them and said to Mary his mother, 'You see this child: he is destined for the fall and for the rising of many in Israel, destined to be a sign that is rejected—and a sword will pierce your own soul too—so that the secret thoughts of many may be laid bare'." (Lk 2:33-35). Yes, Mary had to pay a great price to live out her complete dedication to her Son, Jesus. She drank deeply from the chalice of suffering. It is good to know that we have a mother who understands through her own existential experience the suffering involved in the following of Jesus. We will never be asked to suffer as deeply as she did. But whatever the degree of our suffering, we know that we can approach a mother who has suffered before us. We know that she will understand.

Of all the tremendous gifts with which God has blessed us, certainly the gift of the beautiful woman, Mary, is one of the most precious. In our present day, just as when she lived in Nazareth, she is real and portrays the same desirable and beautiful qualities so necessary for today's world. We are by far the poorer if we make no attempt to relate to her in our lives. Perhaps her qualities and beauty can be best summed up in her own expression concerning the source of her strength and beauty and greatness: "My soul proclaims the greatness of the Lord and my spirit exults in God my savior; because he has looked upon his lowly handmaid. Yes, from this day forward all generations will call me blessed, for the Almighty has done great things for me." (Lk 1:46-49).

14

Loneliness

Modern man is in a special way subject to loneliness. His technological age has established an atmosphere in which the process of alienation can find fertile ground. Consequently, modern man has to make a special effort not to become alienated from himself and from his fellowman.

Contemporary man can become alienated from his true self, from his own personal core, because he can so easily become just a cog in the great technological and economic machine of our day. He has a slot to fill, a job to do, a task to accomplish. The economic structure is often more interested in the fact that the job is accomplished, rather than in the person who accomplishes it. It does not matter too much whether this or that person performs the task. The important thing is that things get done. This is the way our contemporary business and industrial complex often looks upon its labor force. Because modern man breathes in this atmosphere day after day, he has to be on his guard that he does not begin to look upon himself in the same fashion—as an impersonal functionary who fills the slot, who gets the job done. When he surrenders to this dehumanizing process, he feels a sense of loneliness, for he is being alienated or separated from his true self. He becomes alienated from his inner personal core with all its uniqueness and mystery, with its powers of creativity, wonder and inquisitiveness.

Contemporary man also often feels a sense of alienation and a concomitant loneliness in reference to his fellowman, especially in urban areas. This type of alienation and loneliness is closely connected with that which emanates from the kind of work structure just described. People of our age have gathered together in huge centers of population to serve the industrial complex. Whether or not they come to know and love one another doesn't seem to matter too much in many instances. Urban man serves the economic structure, and if he is not careful the structure can easily make him a less loving person, one who is not too interested in the people who daily surround him. The more people there are who succumb to this temptation, the greater becomes the atmosphere of collective estrangement and loneliness. This increased collective estrangement, in turn, creates more instances of apartment buildings filled with people who are strangers to one another. This collective alienation increases the number of populated city streets which become more crowded, but less friendly. It increases the number of business offices where people become more efficient, but less personally interested in the people with whom they work.

The Christian, especially the urban Christian, must compensate for this contemporary atmosphere of alienation and loneliness. He must strive to keep fresh in his consciousness the truths of Christ which will enable him to cope properly with the situation. He must bring to his work a sense of being a collaborator with Christ. In his vision of faith he has to penetrate the surface of things. He has to strive to realize that with faith's vision he can remain human, he can control a sense of alienation, a sense of loneliness in his work, despite the impersonalism with which he may be surrounded. His Christic vision tells him that this work is important, that it all does matter, that it is helping to continue God's creative and redemptive effort.

The Christian must also cut through the barriers of alienation in reference to his fellowman. The loneliness resulting from the forces of alienation in today's society can be considerably lessened if one has a deep love of people. This deep love prompts the Christian to look upon everyone he meets with a sense of wonder and respect for that individual's person, for his uniqueness, for his mystery. This deep love for people would make the Christian want to be friends with everybody, if the barriers of time, space, energy, and personality differences did not make this impossible. This deep love for others enables the Christian to feel a sense of communion with the throngs of people in a busy downtown area, in a filled concert hall, or in a packed sports arena. True, he will never know these thousands personally, but he knows that he and they have the same heavenly Father. He knows that it has been the same blood of Christ that has touched both him and them. These, then, are a few examples of how the truth of Christ can help us to diminish the atmosphere of collective alienation and loneliness of today's society.

There are many other forms of loneliness which are common to man regardless of the age in which he lives. There is the loneliness of crucial decision-making. One can seek advice. He can weigh and consider the opinions of others which collectively cover the entire spectrum of possibilities. But ultimately the one responsible for the decision has to make it within the lonely depths of his own being. It is his decision and his alone. No one else is responsible. Those holding authority often experience this kind of loneliness, and the greater their authority, and the more extensive the ramifications of their decisions, the greater can be their loneliness.

There is the loneliness those about to undergo serious surgery experience. They can receive comfort and support from loved ones, but ultimately there is an aloneness which remains, the aloneness which is the realization that there may never be another tomorrow. Those who are aware that they have a disease or illness which will end in death experience a similar loneliness, one which can be intensified because of the slow approach of the end. The person realizes that the ultimate point of his life is upon him. He may receive great consolation and attention from his loved ones. A priest may be constantly available for the administration of the sacraments. But ultimately the person knows that alone he must pass through the portals of death. No one can accompany him.

One of the deepest forms of loneliness is the loss in death of one who has been deeply loved. How many there are who have experienced this suffering. A husband loses his wife, and he feels that part of his very self has left him, never again to return during this mortal life. Past memories fill his days and the realization that the experiences of those memories will never be repeated can cause a crushing sense of being alone. Or a young child suddenly loses both parents, and the sense of loneliness is overwhelming. The burden is a heavy one for such small shoulders to carry.

We can also experience loneliness because of the values we believe in. It can so happen that even those who are close to us do not always hold the same values as ourselves. They do not always have the same perspective of life as we. To stand by one's beliefs and convictions in such situations can stir up feelings of loneliness which can go so deep at times that some cannot endure them. They prefer to compromise their values so that they can join the crowd. This is particularly true of adolescents.

Closely connected with the above kind of loneliness is that which results from being misunderstood by those whom we love very dearly. At certain times we will cause hurt and misunderstanding precisely because we are trying to do God's will. We can hurt friends, parents and others because they do not understand that we are acting in a certain way because we feel God's will is asking this or that of us. This can cause a deeper hurt within ourselves precisely because we are hurting those we love. But we know we have to embrace God's will. Amid all this hurt and misunderstanding, a deep sense of aloneness can afflict us.

There is a type of aloneness which we may call creative. Artists, musicians, writers, scholars, are the kind of persons who especially must be willing to bear with this category of loneliness. They need a considerable amount of time to be alone with their particular pursuits. Out of this creative solitude have come some of the greatest testimonies of man's thrust towards the good, the true, and the beautiful. But since all of us should be creative in our own way, there should be some of this creative aloneness in the life of each of us. All of us need a certain solitude to re-create ourselves. We have to refurbish the sense of our uniqueness. We have to refresh our vision which tells us that this uniqueness means that we bring a sense of creativity to whatever we do. We share a particular kind of work or profession with many others. We have the same human nature as all other men. The Christian life is basically the same for us as it is for all the other members of the People of God. But in all those instances we still are uniquely different. Our own creative uniqueness, then, affects our work, our existence as human persons, our existence as a Christian.

There is a common form of loneliness which revolves around human love. There are countless numbers of people who are lonely, sometimes deeply so, because they feel there is a lack of human love in their lives. This can take many forms. A child can feel unloved by his parents. They seem more interested in social status and making money than in him, and he feels so alone and unwanted. A wife, who loves her husband deeply, gradually perceives his love for her to grow cool, and eventually it seems to fade altogether. Life for her which once seemed so gay and filled with promise in the early years of married love, now becomes covered with a heavy shadow of loneliness.

The reality of human love causes loneliness not only in those who feel a lack of love in their lives. It can also cause loneliness in those persons who are united in the deepest bonds of love. Separation from one another is one factor which can cause this loneliness. There is that ultimate separation as far as this life is concerned which is death itself. This radical separation and the loneliness it causes we have already described. But even while those who love one another are still both alive, there is a sense of aloneness caused at times by the thought that death some day will probably take one before the other. There are also lesser forms of separation caused by military service, by one's work or profession, and the like. There is that very painful and frustrating kind of loneliness born from separation which thrusts itself into the lives of a few. It is the loneliness resulting from the separation caused by psychic illness. When a loved one withdraws into the land of the mentally ill, there is a deep sense of loneliness because of the inability to communicate properly with the loved one. The more serious the mental disturbance and the more prolonged, the deeper is this loneliness.

There are other dimensions of loneliness caused by the fact that two persons love one another. There can be a sense of aloneness caused by the fact that here below there can never be that perfect kind of union which true lovers desire either very explicitly or more implicitly. Whether it is the case of man and wife, or parent and child, or friend and friend, the situation is basically the same. Because of various factors, there will never be a perfect union of two persons in this life. The perfect union will occur only in eternity. When we realize this fact, and when we are existentially experiencing it, we are aware of a kind of aloneness. Paradoxically, then, not to love and not to be loved cause loneliness, but to love and to be loved also are sources of particular facets of aloneness. But there is this difference between the two—the loneliness born of love is the one we would all prefer.

There is that radical experience of loneliness which arises out of one's own individuality. Man is a social being and in so many ways he is aided in the achievement of his temporal and eternal destinies through the help he receives from others. But ultimately each of us has to face life in a certain aloneness before God. In the deep mystery of our free wills each of us has the alternative of choosing God or rejecting Him. Each of us has the alternative of being a mediocre Christian or of being a completely dedicated one. No one can make these radical decisions for us. We make these decisions, to repeat, as social beings, and in this sense certainly not as isolated individuals. But still we are individuals, and our individuality brings an inevitable aloneness with it as we face life, as we decide for Christ or fail to do so.

We have discussed some of the various types of loneliness which man may encounter. The Christian should realize that he is to make his Christianity relevant to the experience of loneliness as well as to everything else in his life. For there are certain kinds of loneliness which can be eliminated or diminished by incorporating various Christian truths more dynamically into our lives. For example, loneliness can be occasioned because we are not loving persons to a sufficient degree, or because we do not properly open ourselves to the love others want to give us. Then there are those forms of loneliness which are inevitable, or which result from the fact that we are precisely being what we should be. Here again Christian principles and practices can help. These allow us to relate to the loneliness properly and afford us the strength to bear with the suffering involved. If we are the Christians we should be, we can, consequently, cope with loneliness properly, and actually grow because of it as we look ahead to eternity where loneliness will be no more, and where its tears and all other tears will be forever wiped away.

15

Psychological Dimensions
of the Spiritual Life

We have acknowledged the fact that the spiritual life
of man is his total human life as lived in the Spirit.
There is nothing authentically human which can be
omitted in a treatment of the spiritual life. The more
essential any dimension of his human life, the more important role this dimension plays in the spiritual life of
man.

Over recent decades increasing degrees of attention
have been given to the psychological make-up or dimension of man. We have come to realize the immense importance of psychological health to man if he is to live
a happy, fulfilled, or even adequate human life. The
contemporary emphasis has been placed on psychological health in man as a positive quality, one in which
a person can continually grow. The emphasis is not on
a mere absence of diseased or abnormal states.

Many theorists have attempted to spell out for us the
characteristics which are essential to the psychologically
healthy man and have supplied us with an abundance
of specific qualities. Though these qualities are often
stated in varying terminology, a certain common set of

general characteristics is apparent. Recognizing the role these qualities play in the relationship between the spiritual and psychological dimensions of the Christian person, we will here treat of these common general characteristics of the psychologically healthy person. While recognizing the fact that any complete treatment of this dimension of man is prohibited by the nature of the present work, we will develop several aspects of this dimension which are pertinent to the spiritual life of man.

To be whole as a man in a psychological sense, each person must develop and grow in three basic areas. Man must recognize and accept reality, the reality of the world, of his own particular environment, of the circumstances of his own life. He must not only recognize and accept this reality, but also deal with it effectively. Secondly, man must know and accept himself as the unique reality which he is. Finally, in accord with the reality of his social nature, man must accept and relate with other persons. To the degree that man effectively deals with these three aspects of reality, to that degree can he be considered psychologically healthy.

Man exists in the physical world. He also exists in a particular "little world" or environment of his own. Both of these realities, by their very existence, present to man certain circumstances with which he must come to terms if he is to live his life in harmony with reality. Adrian Van Kaam, in treating this aspect of psychological health states: "Existentially speaking, however, the most fundamental characteristic of the true personality is constant readiness to respond fully to the demands of reality."[1] While we are aware of the extreme state of

[1] Adrian Van Kaam, *Religion and Personality* (New Jersey: Prentice-Hall, Inc., 1964), p. 81.

psychological illness termed psychosis in which a person has lost contact with reality, we would here prefer to discuss the less severe yet more commonly occurring states in which one refuses to acknowledge reality. These states exist in varying degrees of severity.

We have all met in others, or, in moments of honesty, been aware of in ourselves, the attitude which ignores reality. Obvious examples of this attitude exist in abundance in our everyday lives. Teachers may recall frequent experiences with parents who refuse to accept their child's lack of ability, aptitude, or the reality of his misbehavior. Physicians and nurses can often recount numerous patients who refuse to believe reports of serious illness. From a slightly different viewpoint, we are aware of those who only believe what they experience themselves. The war in Vietnam with all its horror and tragedy, though brought into their homes daily through the news media, does not actually exist for them. They cannot see how it touches their own lives, and until it does so, they treat it as though it did not exist. Perhaps quite vivid portrayals of this example have been noted in families which were suddenly very much aware of and involved with the war when a son was inducted into the military service. This type of example can be multiplied over and over, as in the cases of violence being experienced in our own cities, or in reports of untold numbers of starving people in countries throughout the world. Various examples of wrongdoing and sinful behavior with the concomitant ignoring of any consequences to such behavior, whether these consequences be in the temporal or spiritual order, could also be cited.

In all of these examples listed above, and the list could be extended indefinitely, we can see that the objective reality is one thing, and that the particular subjective view of the reality held by the person described is something else. The state of psychological health exists when these two qualifying aspects of reality become one. This is experienced when there is no difference between what actually exists and what the individual person perceives as existing, whether this reality be in the realm of things, circumstances, activities, or any other form reality may take. It is important here to reiterate that we are not here dealing with those states of distortion of reality which are due to illness which is beyond the person's control. Rather, for whatever may be the reason or cause of their difficulty, we are here concerning ourselves with those distortions which could be corrected by the person involved. In these instances, man's distortion of reality cannot be excused by an outright severe psychological illness which may prevent him from true perception. Some of these factors causing misperception may be based in the psychological unconscious. Others fall within the realm of conscious free choice and control. Often it is difficult, if not possible, to make distinctions between the roles played by these causative factors. Let us consider the example stated above of the parent refusing to accept the reality of his child's misbehavior. To acknowledge that one's child has behaved badly may be not only to acknowledge *that* fact, but to acknowledge simultaneously one's own inaptitude as a parent. For one parent this may be a matter of fearfulness regarding one's own inadequacies; for another it may be purely a matter of pride. In regard to the examples of lack of involvement, as in the war situation, the causative factors may fall within the realm of one's taking the least painful and least bothersome route. To concern oneself with the plight of those starving or those causing or being subjected to violence would be too painful, would demand too much from a person. Therefore, it becomes far easier when one is not directly touched by these realities to act as though they did not exist. This same reasoning could be applied to the situation involving outright sinful behavior or wrongdoing. Behavior of this sort says, "If I act as though the reality of the consequences of my sinfulness does not exist, I can behave as I wish and don't have to worry about it."

One can readily see the outcome of such modes of ignoring reality, of not allowing the subjective and objective realities to meet. By acting in such a manner a man would be thwarting his own welfare. It is as though he were attempting to cure a disease by using a remedy which provided only a feeling of well-being without in any way affecting the reality of the disease. While man can always expect some distortion of objective reality simply as a result of his own subjectivity, it is obviously quite important that he strive always to narrow the gap between the two. We know that man's behavior is dependent upon his perception of reality, and reality does exist in itself and can be known by man. Therefore, any time man acts contrary to objective reality, his behavior is less than human.

As was mentioned previously, there can be a variety of factors which are at the root of such behavior. Often the ignoring of the reality can be seen to be a utilization of the mechanism of denial. This is the technique used by one's ego whereby it refuses to allow awareness of some unpleasant or threatening aspect of external reality. This mechanism clearly involves a defective or incomplete appraisal of reality. If this should be used by an adult to any great extent, it would be a sign of illness. As has been demonstrated by our examples above, the particular reality denied by the individual provided more unpleasantness or threat than he was willing or able to accept. It is apparent that a state of health would ordinarily involve the acceptance of reality as it exists.

The problem of the denial of reality, of whatever degree, has definite bearing upon the spiritual life of man. As in all of salvation history, man is to work out his salvation in the medium of reality. The events and circumstances of man's world or environment provide the matrix in which his life is to develop, and this obviously includes his spiritual life. As the earthly life of Jesus was lived out in a particular time and environment with all its difficulties and hardships, so it is for man. Jesus accomplished His mission in life, not by ignoring the events and circumstances of the time, but by accepting them, involving Himself in them, and working toward their improvement. In fact, He became so involved that He eventually became a victim of the very circumstances of the day. Because men were not what they should have been, He was put to death. This fact in itself ought to provide some direction or support to modern man. It is not only the circumstances and events of life with which we agree that we are to accept. Reality for us always will contain a great deal which is painful or difficult, many things we would prefer to have otherwise, and even things which are evil. Things could always be better as long as we are on earth. But if we dealt only with what is according to our wishes, we would be dealing with very little of that which constitutes the whole of reality.

As has been stated, Jesus has left us an example. Apparently He felt it quite important not to live the life of a hermit, although He would give others the vocation of a hermit. Because He wanted to give an example to all men of all vocations, He chose not to close Himself off from the events of the day. Nor did He deal only with those circumstances of which He approved. He chose to submerge Himself in the Jewish world of His times. He outwardly denounced the behavior of the Pharisees. He ate with sinners. He even accepted the friendship of a prostitute. Often He suffered criticism and denouncement on the head of this involvement, was ridiculed, deserted by some, called insane, or simply was reacted to with indifference. None of this treatment was pleasant for Him. It would have been easier on the natural plane to close His eyes to all that was evil or unpleasant and live a simple, quiet life off on His own. We feel the point is quite obvious. As Jesus' mission was accomplished, not in spite of, but in the very midst of His involvement with reality, so it is for man. Not by ignoring reality when it is arduous or hard to bear, but by working through it to the best of his ability, can man accomplish his own mission. Life often deals painful blows to every man, but it is only by working through these difficult and trying times that man can grow both psychologically and spiritually. Growth in any sphere is never a product of closing one's eyes to reality. In describing his own criteria for emotional maturity which he sees as "life goals if one wants to achieve the most of his own personality", Dr. Roy W. Menninger, the noted psychiatrist, first lists "having the ability to deal constructively with reality".[2] Scripture bids us do likewise if we are to attain spiritual growth and maturity. In

[2] Roy W. Menninger, M.D., "Emotional Maturity". In Arthur Le-Clair, *Wonder in the Wild*. (Carthagena, Ohio: Messenger Press, 1969), p. 88.

approaching those aspects of the real world which are painful to us, from which we would prefer to flee, we can call to mind the words of St. James: "My brothers, you will always have your trials but, when they come, try to treat them as a happy privilege; you understand that your faith is only put to the test to make you patient, but patience too is to have its practical results so that you will become fully-developed, complete, with nothing missing." (Jm 1:2-4).

There are various consequences which necessarily flow from ignoring reality. In several of the examples cited above it is apparent that because I ignore or remain distant from certain realities, my brothers in the family of men suffer. This can certainly be seen to be true in the cases of starvation, war, and violence. Some effort on the part of each man must be expended to alleviate these problems in our society. Their existence cannot be denied, and any individual man's lack of involvement with these problems hinders their solution to the detriment of all mankind. In the final section of this chapter we will further treat a person's relations with his fellow man.

Finally, it is conceivable to see the acceptance of reality as it exists as the midpoint on a continuum. At one end of this continuum is a strict idealism which accepts only those aspects of reality which are not too painful. At the opposite extreme is the state which is quite pessimistic in outlook and sees only the evils of reality. It is apparent that a healthy state is that which can stand in the middle and balance the contributions of the two extremes. While enjoying the good gifts one does not forget to accept those which are unpleasant and arduous. This same continuum model can also illustrate several other aspects of the phase of good psychological health we are discussing. This state of health can usually be found as the balance or midpoint between two extremes. We see this with the continuum of emotion and reason. While both reason and emotion are good human capacities, to regulate one's behavior solely upon one or the other can indicate a denial or absence of knowledge or respect for man's nature. Man was created with both gifts. Both are meant to be of benefit to him in his human life. In our society, however, it has become popular to assign greater emotionality to women and rational thinking to men. For example, we are all aware of the accepted standard in our society which looks upon a man's crying as a sign of weakness. It should be quite obvious to us that neither men nor women have cornered the market concerning either of these qualities. The fully human life shows in its maturity a balance between the two. One's rationality or intellectuality is always tempered by a certain degree of emotionality, and vice versa. Good psychological health is always characterized by balance and moderation.

One additional example comes to mind to illustrate this balance necessary for good psychological and spiritual health, and this is the materialism-spiritualism continuum. As a result of early Manichaeistic and Gnostic influences many Christian peoples have been born into the tradition which says that what is material is bad and what is spiritual is good. This is not stated in such specific terms in our world today but the influence remains in much of our behavior. Because the human body is quite obviously material, it was and is held in suspicion. Spirituality too often stressed the denial of what the human body desired. Many forms of human enjoyment were also seen as evil. Only what was seen as good for man's soul was to be pursued, and spirituality at times almost took the form of a hatred for what is human. Today, in an attempt to show contempt for the earlier error, many are now becoming involved in the error at the opposite extreme on the continuum. We are all aware of persons who exemplify both extremes. We know the playboys, certain business men, and others who are so involved in material reality that they have no time for their spiritual life. Conversely we know of those so involved in "praying for souls" and concentrating on their own "spiritual welfare" that they have no time for persons directly around them or the demands of their material world. Only by a balance of these two extremes can man deal with life in the way in which it actually exists.

We can conclude the discussion of this aspect of good psychological health and emotional maturity by summarizing our recommendations. Reality must be accepted and dealt with as it exists. The most healthy way we can do this is to function with balance and moderation, avoiding the extremes we have discussed.

We have stated that the second basic area in which each person must develop and grow pertains to man in himself. Man must know and accept himself as the unique reality which he is. In his psychiatric text, Dr. Charles Hofling makes the following comments pertinent to the dimension of psychological health we are here discussing: "For the human organism there is of course an inner, as well as an outer, reality. Therefore, another significant corollary involves the taking of this inner reality into consideration (self-knowledge). It is typical of the mature, well-adjusted individual that his actions be in reasonable accord with his inner reality."[3]

[3] Charles K. Hofling, M.D., *Textbook of Psychiatry for Medical Practice,* Second Edition (Philadelphia: J. B. Lippincott Company, 1968), p. 36.

In beginning our discussion of this dimension of mental health it is interesting to note that Jesus Himself took this aspect as an accepted fact. He was speaking of the importance of loving one's neighbor, but the model He gave for this love was that which a person already is to have for himself. "You must love your neighbor as yourself." (Mt 22:39).

Basic to love for anyone or anything is knowledge. It is commonly held that love is impossible without a certain prior knowledge of that which is loved. So it is with self-knowledge and self-love. Man must make every effort to know himself. We have all seen persons who apparently have little self-knowledge and either underestimate or overestimate their abilities. We know the employee who pushes himself one step beyond his ability for optimal performance. We know the employee who never realizes his potential for advancement. We have seen the person who seeks and accepts degrees of responsibility which are beyond his personal talents. And we have seen the person with great potential for leadership and responsibility hold back because he feels incapable. Each of these instances, bearing the real possibility of poor judgment after adequate consideration, illustrates poor self-knowledge.

Each man, as the unique individual that he is, has been endowed with a certain repertory of talents, abilities, characteristics, and a personality structure. He lives, he grows, he reacts, he feels, he performs, he thinks —all within the unique framework of his own person. He has many basic dimensions of his nature in common with all men, but the way in which he lives out his life in every aspect is uniquely his own. A circumstance one person may shrug off with indifference can deeply sadden or irritate another. One person may be very moved by the gratitude of a gift and another may accept it as his due. One person cries at personal hurt and another acts out in anger.

To determine why these differences occur is beyond the scope of this book. What is important here is that they do exist in each individual. In order to love oneself properly, a man must learn as much as possible about himself. It has been said that each man exists in three distinct ways: as the person he thinks he is in himself, as the person others see him to be, and as the person he actually is. While it is impossible to ever bring these three persons completely into unity, it is healthy to try to approach this unity as much as possible. At the foundation of such an approximation is self-knowledge. Only when man knows himself as he truly is can he live his life as the unique person he was created to be. Each man, as the possessor of his own unique characteristics, is meant to live out his life utilizing the uniqueness of his own traits. No one is meant to be anyone else.

It is apparent that it is only by a true knowledge of himself as the basis of his life that man can hope to live with any success. If he sees himself in a false light and behaves accordingly he is ordinarily geared for failure as in the examples cited above. He who sees himself as a great salesman, while lacking the natural qualities of salesmanship, misses many opportunities for fruitful living. Not only does he fail to sell his product, but he also misses all the joy and satisfaction that would come to him from a job well done in a field for which he is suited. Similar difficulties would occur whether he overestimated, underestimated, or poorly estimated himself and his own abilities. As has been brought out in the chapter on personal uniqueness, only by living one's life in accord with a true view of oneself can man fulfill his role as the unique member of the People of God he was created to be. This takes into account his whole person, his uniqueness in his totality as a person. Only by such a knowledge of himself can man come to any practice of the virtue of humility. For, as has also been stated, humility is truth.

This self-knowledge can be acquired in several ways. Dr. Sidney Jourard, an American psychologist, has said that a person can only come to know himself by disclosing himself to another.[4] It is only in seeing something of oneself reflected back from another person that that aspect of oneself becomes known. We all are probably aware of some aspects of ourselves which became quite vivid to us in this manner. The topic of relationship with others, upon which this bears, will be further treated in the final portion of this chapter.

A further step in self-knowledge must be added to the above, and that is the necessity of reflection. One can be exposed to certain dimensions of himself over and over again, but without a certain degree of reflection and assessment this knowledge can never become real to him. In the event that the picture of himself he receives is distorted, he can, through such honest reflection, come to some degree of truth regarding himself. By this same reflection he can simply become aware of his own behavior, the way in which he acts when alone, his own views of reality, his beliefs, his goals, his desires, his feelings towards others. All of this information, if perceived with some degree of clarity and truthfulness, can add to his own knowledge of himself.

The final point to be made regarding this aspect of

[4] Cf Sidney M. Jourard, *The Transparent Self* (New York: Van Nostrand, 1964), p. 10.

psychological health is that of self-acceptance and true self-love. This can be seen as a natural follow-up or necessary sequel to the first point made in this chapter, the acceptance of reality. Each person is a reality in the uniqueness of his own personhood. As has been stated, man is to work out his salvation, not by ignoring reality, or wishing things were other than they are, but by accepting what is and developing his life through this medium. The man who knows himself to be prone to periods of self-pity and melancholia will strive a little harder to think positive thoughts regarding himself and be joyful. He who knows he has a tendency to neglect others' needs, or to gossip, or to force his own way, is a step closer to the elimination of these faults than he who is not aware of them. It should be easy to see, then, that acceptance of oneself does not merely mean that one is to remain satisfied with himself. One can accept the fact, rather than deny or ignore it, that he is less than perfect in every facet of his being. Yet, in real self-love, he will move from this knowledge to seek his own good and betterment by self-renewal or self-improvement. In this way he is moving toward the state desired for him by God: "You must therefore be perfect just as your heavenly Father is perfect." (Mt 5:48).

As a final support to the importance of the point we have been making in regard to man's knowledge and acceptance of himself, let us quote John W. Gardner: "Research in psychology and psychiatry has shown the extent to which mental health is bound up in a reasonably objective view of the self, in accessibility of the self to consciousness, and in acceptance of the self."[5]

[5] John W. Gardner, *Self-Renewal* (New York: Harper & Row, 1963), p. 13.

The third and final characteristic of the psychologically healthy man with which we will deal is that springing from his nature as a social being. Men were not placed upon earth in separation from each other. In the Old Testament we were told by God that we were not created in isolation. "Yahweh God said, 'It is not good that the man should be alone. I will make him a helpmate.'" (Gn 2:18). This, then, man's social nature, is the foundation upon which we build our final dimension of health. Man must accept other persons and relate with them.

Time and time again throughout the New Testament we are told just how we are to relate to each other. "You must love your neighbor as yourself." (Mt 22:39). "I give you a new commandment: love one another; just as I have loved you, you also must love one another. By this love you have for one another, everyone will know that you are my disciples." (Jn 13:34-35). "This has taught us love—that he gave up his life for us; and we, too, ought to give up our lives for our brothers. If a man who was rich enough in this world's goods saw that one of his brothers was in need, but closed his heart to him, how could the love of God be living in him? My children, our love is not to be just words or mere talk, but something real and active." (I Jn 3:16-18). Examples and quotations such as these could be further extended. In reading the New Testament we certainly come to realize that love is a very central issue. It is as if Jesus and the inspired writers, realizing the importance and, at the same time, difficulty of such love, wanted to stress it for us by repetition. In this way it is impossible for us to miss the point.

In discussing this facet of man's emotional health and well-being it is interesting to trace the psychological

development of a man. According to what we are told
by psychologists, an infant is born totally involved with
himself. He is the center of his universe. Everything he
does is aimed at bringing pleasure to himself. He reacts
vigorously if he perceives any threat or frustration to
his own pleasure. When he is hungry, or wet, or uncomfortable in any way, he desires the immediate alleviation
of his perceived distress by crying loudly and with
great demand. He can be said to be naturally and totally selfish, with thought for none other than himself.
Even the most important "other", his mother, is perceived by him as indistinct from himself, as part of
himself.

The natural stages of psychological growth and development show the infant moving from this stage of
extreme selfishness through successive stages in which
his orientation is to shift gradually towards others. While
never losing a true love and concern for himself and his
own well-being, the emotionally mature man can let
the needs of others supersede his own. He can say no
to himself in order that more pleasure be brought to
others than to himself. Many factors can be seen to
enter into this development. Even the small child soon
learns that to be desired as a playmate, to get along with
others on even the most superficial level, it is necessary
at times to put others before oneself. Emotional maturity is reached, then, when the person is able to control
himself so that his own wishes and desires need not
always be fulfilled before those of others. When he
reaches this stage, he should be so able to appreciate
the beauty, uniqueness, abilities, or qualities of another
that he can relate with others in sincere sharing.

We have seen that in the natural sphere of man's
healthy emotional growth one develops from a total
involvement with self outward to involvement with

others. There is an interesting facet of this development for Christian man. What Jesus asks of His followers, if they desire to be good Christians, is quite obviously that which is in accord with good mental health. In stressing the importance of love, He is, in effect, saying, "Go out of yourself to others. Learn to say no to yourself so that you can say yes to your brother. Be able to put your neighbor first. When you have accomplished this, then not only will you be growing psychologically, but you will also be abounding in spiritual health, since love will be the basis of your behavior."

The manner in which this love and relatedness is to be carried out and lived is often misunderstood. We have a tendency to look for outstanding and extraordinary manifestations of love, or to look upon it solely in the "candy and flowers" framework. And yet, the way spelled out for us in the writings of St. Paul seems totally to ignore both of these methods and states some very ordinary ways of showing love. This is not to say that love cannot be periodically manifested in outstanding and beautiful ways. The point we are making is that real love is shown, not only in the flamboyance of extraordinary demonstrations, but most especially in the unsung, day by day, difficult aspects of living. "Love is always patient and kind; it is never jealous; love is never boastful or conceited; it is never rude or selfish; it does not take offense, and is not resentful. Love takes no pleasure in other people's sins but delights in the truth; it is always ready to excuse, to trust, to hope, and to endure whatever comes." (I Co 13:4-7).

In an examination of this list of love's characteristics it is quite evident that it is composed of the substance of our daily lives. We do not have to sit back and wait for a certain person to come along in order to love as St. Paul directs. We cannot help but be reminded of

Jesus' own explanation when He was asked to indicate who was one's neighbor. We know this question followed on His directive to love one's neighbor as one loves himself. His response was the story of the Good Samaritan (Lk 10:29-37), in which love is shown to an unknown person. This story ought, then, to leave no doubt that we are to love all our fellowmen. Of course, due to personality variables and life circumstances, and simply the mystery of loving, there will be certain persons with whom we will share love more deeply than others. But the basic rule of loving is that this is to be the fundamental relationship of the human race. As is so often demonstrated, the elements of good psychological health can go hand in hand with the elements of spiritual health. However, while the spiritual growth and development from self to others parallels that of psychological growth, they do not necessarily occur simultaneously. This can be accomplished, but only by the individual who loves in the spirit of Christ's command.

One further point must be acknowledged here. Going out to others can be performed in a manner that is not even conducive to psychological growth. A salesman who treats his client with great kindness and concern solely to make a sale is not even exhibiting healthy psychological behavior. Nor is the young girl showing healthy psychological behavior who is outwardly friendly and gracious to her classmates only for the sake of popularity. In both instances they are merely using the other persons to achieve their own desires and ends. This, it can be seen, is in one sense a return to an infantile stage of psychological development.

We have stated that psychological health is of immense importance to man's living a happy, fulfilled, even adequate life in the world, to his being at home with himself, and to his living in authentic relationship with others. We have attempted to show three basic dimensions of this health—the necessity of the acceptance of reality, the knowledge and acceptance of oneself, and the acceptance and relatedness with others. Man is not a divided being within himself. In this instance as in many others his basic unity is apparent. He cannot be whole in any one aspect or dimension of his humanity without this affecting every other dimension. By the same rule, he cannot be seriously lacking in any one dimension without this affecting the others. This is the point we have tried to make in this chapter. Man is one, and his spirituality will often have great dependence on and interaction with the psychological dimension of his nature. Consequently, he must strive to attain the fullest development possible in every facet of his being, the psychological, the spiritual, and every other dimension.

Here we should make an important observation. What about those who are afflicted with a neurosis or even psychosis? Not all would agree here. What seems to be the better opinion makes a distinction between what may be called a total holiness, one which manifests itself throughout one's entire being including the psychological dimension, and what might be called essential holiness, a kind which resides in the depths of the person, but which does not manifest itself in all dimensions as it ideally should. This type of holiness can exist in those who are mentally ill. They must take the reasonable means to cure and control the illness. If they do this, they can be assured that a deep Christian or spiritual life is possible for them also. Yet the ideal is that the Christian life of grace manifests itself through a human life which is psychologically healthy.

16

Suffering
—and Resurrection Now

The reality of suffering has perennially been a problem for many. Some apparently are tempted to give up their religion when intense suffering enters their lives. They find it difficult to understand how the goodness of God would permit such suffering. Others make every effort to flee suffering in each and every instance. They may seek escape in a hedonistic pursuit of pleasure, in alcoholism, in drugs, or in a morbid use of defense mechanisms which results in a neurotic or psychotic condition. But theirs is a fruitless task. They cannot completely escape all suffering any more than they can flee from their own shadows. Ultimately, they will suffer more precisely because they are immaturely trying to escape pain. There are others who become bitter because of suffering. Even though they once may have been the most attractive personalities, they become changed through their bitterness into persons who tend to repel everyone they encounter.

The real tragedy concerning suffering is not that there is so much of it. Rather the real tragedy is that so much of it is wasted. When suffering is properly related to, it helps make a person more beautiful, a greater lover of God and man, more capable of fulfilling his unique role in life. Christianity provides us with a proper vision of suffering. In the reflection of faith we can see in the course of salvation history the positive purpose for which God uses suffering.

In God's dealings with men suffering is intimately linked with the pattern of death-resurrection which, in turn, constitutes one of the great themes of salvation history. We see this pattern of death-resurrection at the heart of Old Testament history. The Jewish people, under the leadership of Moses, experienced death-resurrection as they were formed into the people of the covenant, Yahweh's people. In the great Exodus event, they escaped Egyptian slavery, went on to Mt. Sinai where the covenant was ratified, and then progressed to the Promised Land. As they were formed into Yahweh's people as members of the Mosaic covenant, a religious transition was taking place. The Jews were passing over to a higher level of religious existence, to a more intimate union with God.

Death-resurrection was involved in this religious transition. To become people of the covenant, to remain so, and to grow in the life of the covenant, demanded a mystical or spiritual death. The Jews had to be willing to pay a price. They had to endure a spiritual dying. They had to be willing to bear with that which was hard and difficult in covenant life. They had to be willing to die to that which was not according to Yahweh's will. But this mystical death had a very positive purpose. It was directed at life in the covenant and at growth in that life. In other words, this spiritual death was aimed at resurrection.

Christ perfectly fulfilled the Old Testament theme

of death-resurrection. In doing so He too was experiencing a religious transition. He was passing over gradually, and then definitively in death, to a new kind of religious existence, to the life of His resurrection. He achieved this new life not only for His own humanity, but for all of mankind. To achieve this new life of resurrection, Christ was willing to pay the price. He was willing to suffer, yes, even unto death. The extent of His sufferings is graphically and poignantly described in the book of Isaiah: "As the crowds were appalled on seeing him—so disfigured did he look that he seemed no longer human—so will the crowds be astonished at him. . . . Without beauty, without majesty (we saw him), no looks to attract our eyes; a thing despised and rejected by men, a man of sorrows and familiar with suffering, a man to make people screen their faces; he was despised and we took no account of him. And yet ours were the sufferings he bore, ours the sorrows he carried . . . he was pierced through for our faults, crushed for our sins. . . . Harshly dealt with, he bore it humbly, he never opened his mouth, like a lamb that is led to the slaughter-house, like a sheep that is dumb before its shearers never opening its mouth." (Is 52:14-53:7).

That it had to be this way, that the only way Christ could have achieved resurrection was through suffering and death, was pointed out by Jesus Himself as He appeared to the two disciples on the road to Emmaus: "Then he said to them, 'You foolish men! So slow to believe the full message of the prophets! Was it not ordained that the Christ should suffer and so enter into his glory?' Then, starting with Moses and going through all the prophets, he explained to them the passages throughout the scriptures that were about himself." (Lk 24: 25-27).

Christ has structured the Christian life by the way He Himself lived as man while upon earth. It is obvious, then, that the pattern of death-resurrection must be at the heart of the Church's life. The People of God, individually and collectively, are meant to die continually with Christ that they may continually rise with Him. They are being called to pass over in a process of continued religious transition to a greater participation in Christ's resurrection. It is true that our participation in Christ's resurrection will reach its completion only in eternity. Nevertheless, we begin the life of resurrection right here upon this earth, in the here and now of human life, in the midst of joy and pain, success and failure, in the sweat of our brow and in the enjoyment of the good gifts of God. This life of resurrection, our life of grace, is supposed to touch everything authentic about human existence. The Christ-life permeates the entire being of the Christian. He is one graced person. He is supposed to have a sense of growth concerning his here and now life of resurrection. Many Christians seem to have too static a view of the Christian life. They do not seem to have a vital and efficacious realization that the Christian life, or the life of resurrection, is supposed to become more conscious, more experiential, more dynamically relative to daily existence.

We cannot maintain the life of resurrection nor grow in it without a willingness to suffer. This does not mean that we are to be always overwhelmed and heavily burdened by the reality of suffering in our lives. The greater portion of suffering for most Christians seems to be an accumulation of ordinary hardships, difficulties, and pains. At times, though, deep suffering can enter a Christian's life, even suffering of agonizing proportions. During these special periods of suffering the sense of anguish can become so great that the prospect of life continuing becomes an agony in itself. But whether the sufferings of the Christian are of the more ordinary variety or are of the more rare and extreme type, the Christian must be convinced that to relate to suffering properly is to grow in resurrection—and to grow in resurrection for oneself also means an increased capacity to help give resurrection to others.

The reality of suffering can assume many appearances. It can be of a more active variety or of a more passive variety, and under these two general categories there are numerous possibilities. Under the more active type we include those forms of sufferings which are more under our control and depend to a great extent on our own graced initiative. An exercise of Christian self-discipline is one example. This involves suffering, for our natures do not automatically submit to the influence of grace. There are various degrees of hardship, sometimes real struggles, in allowing the Christ-life to control properly our total being with all its sense and spiritual faculties. This attitude of Christian self-discipline demands a dying to that within us whch is not according to Christ. This dying costs nature. It means suffering.

The implementation of Christian renunciation in our lives also involves suffering. There are various reasons for these acts of renunciation as we follow Christ. While not intending to treat all of these, we do offer several different uses of renunciation. One of these is involved in the proper living out of one's vocation or life's work. A priest and religious, for example, give up the great good of marriage. A married person gives up all sorts of freedoms that a single person enjoys. A doctor has to be willing to renounce various outside activities and interests if he is going to meet successfully the challenge of being a competent physician.

Although a committed Christian will joyfully make these acts of renunciation relative to his vocation and life's work, this does not mean that suffering is not experienced. The celibate priest and religious, although they continue with a glad heart to give up the joys and happiness of marriage, can suffer keenly at times over what their celibate state demands of them. A wife and mother can suffer in a similar fashion. She may have given up a highly interesting and rewarding profession in order to marry and rear a family. Despite the fact that she continues to make her sacrifice with joy and love does not mean she cannot at times keenly feel the loss of her career.

Renunciation is also periodically necessary if we are to relate to created goods and values properly as guided by the will of the Creator. It is too much to expect that human nature will always relate properly to creation if it is never denied what it instinctively desires. A good test concerning authenticity in the use of created goods is our willingness to give them up at times, and at such times to go out in faith and love to God as He is in Himself rather than as He is present in His creation. We are meant to experience God in both ways, but, again, if we are never willing to renounce created goods, this is a sign that we are not always seeking God in creation, but rather our selfish selves. We know that this kind of renunciation also causes suffering, and precisely because it does, we have to make the effort to assure that it finds its proper place in our Christian existence.

There is that very prosaic type of suffering involved in the proper living of each day. There is nothing dramatic about this form of pain, and precisely because it seems so uneventful it is very difficult to relate to it properly in a consistent fashion. We may feel on particular occasions that a quick death by martyrdom would be preferable to the daily dying which involves all sorts of little sufferings. But this is a precious type of suffering and to grow in the realization of its importance is a significant sign of spiritual progress. It is a sign that we have the spiritual keenness to comprehend where God so often situates the cross—within the ordinariness of everyday life.

The above are some of the forms of suffering which we may categorize as being of the more active type. They are forms which involve to a considerable degree our active choices. There are other forms of suffering which are of a more passive nature. It may be the case of interior trials involving temptations, or a severe dryness in prayer, or a sense of being abandoned by God, although in reality He may be very close.

Included in this passive kind of suffering is that painful sense of failure in our work, something which all of us experience at least occasionally, and a trial which some have to endure over long periods. It is not a case of not trying, of not being conscientious about one's work. The suffering is present precisely because one is giving his reasonable best, and all that he can see is his lack of success.

Interpersonal relationships involve their particular kind of passive suffering also. Much of our deepest happiness can result from these relationships, but there can be deep pain also. It is precisely because too many are not willing to bear with the suffering involved that there are too few really deep human relationships. For instance, how many marriages fail because one or both parties are unwilling to endure the suffering involved in a constant gift of self?

Experiences of loneliness, especially the loneliness which results from not feeling loved and wanted and appreciated is another common type of passive suffering. We have previously discussed loneliness but it certainly is appropriate to mention it here briefly. This is perhaps one of the more frequent types of suffering that many have to endure.

In our discussion of suffering we should make brief mention of its particular application in today's Church. Generally speaking, everyone is experiencing an unique type of suffering in our contemporary situation because of the deep-rooted renewal and adaptation present in the post-Vatican II Church. There is the pain of uncertainty. Which way is the Spirit leading on this particular issue as opposed to false paths? There is the pain which some experience as they see cherished structures and practices of former days fade into oblivion. There is the suffering of trying to be open to those who think and act so differently than I may. Conversely there is the pain of being misunderstood by others because I may not see the process and purpose of renewal in the same light as they. And we could add to this list of sufferings in today's Church . . . and then add some more.

God is a God of life. All the various types of suffering we have been discussing are meant to lead to a more dynamic existence, to greater resurrection. This life of resurrection centers in love. Consequently, suffering deepens our capacity to integrate more vitally into our Christian existence the four dimensions of Christian love. As we die with Christ in the proper assimilation of suffering, we are rising with Him as Christians more open to God's love, more loving towards Him. We are rising with Christ more capable of loving one another and all men, more open to receiving love from others.

The concept of the life of resurrection is a very appropriate one upon which to end this book. For all the various themes we have been treating are themes of the spiritual life, and the spiritual life is the life of resurrection.

We believe that we live in a time which desparately needs a growing number of Christians of all vocations completely committed to the spiritual life. They must be men and women afire with love of both Christ and their fellowman. They must be deeply spiritual men and women, Christians who live in the Spirit, who have a deep desire to be guided by Him in all things. If they are willing to live in this manner, then they become much more capable of helping the Spirit change the face of the earth. They help Him change it by aiding Him in bringing the earth's Christic image into greater relief. The Christic image is certainly there, but it is still too much covered over. Each of us is daily given the opportunity to help brighten this Christic image of the universe. The manner in which we meet this daily challenge does make a difference.